FEMINISM

DEBORAH CAMERON

P

PROFILE BOOKS

First published in Great Britain in 2018 by
PROFILE BOOKS LTD
3 Holford Yard
Bevin Way
London WC1X 9HD
www.profilebooks.com

A CIP catalogue record for this book is available from the British Library.

ISBN 978 1 78125 837 8

eISBN 978 1 78283 352 9

Designed by Jade Design *www.jadedesign.co.uk*

Printed and bound in Italy by L.E.G.O. S.p.A.

FEMINISM

IDEAS IN **PROFILE**
SMALL INTRODUCTIONS TO BIG TOPICS

ALSO BY DEBORAH CAMERON

The Myth of Mars and Venus: Do Men and Women Really Speak Different Languages?

'Language: a feminist guide', a blog, can be found at www.debuk.wordpress.com

CONTENTS

INTRODUCTION

'We should all be feminists', proclaimed the writer Chimamanda Ngozi Adichie in her celebrated 2014 essay of that name. But a survey conducted in Britain a year later by the polling organisation YouGov found that many women were not so sure. Most agreed that feminism was still needed, but around half said they 'would not call themselves feminists', while one in five regarded the word as an insult.

This ambivalence is nothing new. In 1938 the writer Dorothy L. Sayers gave a lecture to a women's society entitled 'Are women human?' She began with this disclaimer:

> Your Secretary made the suggestion that she thought I must be interested in the feminist movement. I replied – a little irritably, I am afraid – that I was not sure I wanted to 'identify myself', as the phrase goes, with feminism …

This sentiment was common enough at the time to prompt a contemporary of Sayers, the novelist Winifred Holtby, to ask: 'Why, in 1934, are women themselves so often the first to repudiate the movements of the past one hundred and fifty years, which gained for them at least the foundations of political, economic, educational and moral equality?'

Then, as now, one reason for women's reluctance to call themselves feminists was their awareness of the negative stereotype associated with the label: 'feminist' has a long history of being used to disparage women as dour, unfeminine man-haters. In addition, Sayers was writing in the period immediately after women in Britain had gained the right to vote on the same terms as men. Feminism had come to be perceived as old-fashioned and irrelevant, with nothing to say to the post-suffrage generation. (Something similar would happen again 50 years later, as young women in the 1980s and 1990s rejected their mothers' 'Women's Lib', and media commentators proclaimed the advent of the 'post-feminist' era.)

But another answer to Winifred Holtby's question might be that attitudes to feminism tend to vary depending on what 'feminism' is taken to mean. When people use the word 'feminism', they may be talking about any or all of the following:

- Feminism as an idea: as Marie Shear once put it, 'the radical notion that women are people'.
- Feminism as a collective political project: in the words of bell hooks, 'a movement to end sexism, sexist exploitation and oppression'.
- Feminism as an intellectual framework: what the philosopher Nancy Hartsock described as 'a mode of analysis … a way of asking questions and searching for answers'.

These different senses have different histories, and the way they fit together is complicated.

Feminism as an idea is much older than the political movement. In Europe, the beginnings of political feminism are usually located in the late eighteenth century; but a tradition of writing in which women defended their sex against unjust vilification had existed for several centuries before that. The text which inaugurated this tradition was Christine de Pizan's *The Book of the City of Ladies*, written by an educated secular woman in France at the beginning of the fifteenth century. This book made a systematic attempt to rebut the misogynistic arguments about women put forward by male authorities, arguing that the worth of a person does not lie 'in the body according to the sex, but in the perfection of conduct and virtues'. Over the next 400 years, other texts making similar arguments appeared in various parts of Europe. Their authors were relatively few in number, were not part of any collective movement, and did not call themselves feminists (that word did not come into use until the nineteenth century). But they clearly subscribed to 'the radical notion that women are people'. It has been argued that by criticising the masculist bias of what passed, in their time, for knowledge about women, they became, in effect, the first feminist theorists.

Dorothy Sayers also believed that women are people. 'A woman', she wrote, 'is just as much an ordinary human being as a man, with the same individual preferences, and with just as much right to the tastes and preferences of an individual.' But that belief was what made Sayers reluctant to embrace feminism as an organised political movement. 'What is repugnant to every human being', she went on, 'is to be reckoned always as a member of a class and not as an individual person.' This is the paradox at the heart of feminist politics: in order to assert that they are people, just as men are, women must unite on the basis of being women. And since women are a very large, internally diverse group, it has always been difficult to unite them. Feminists may be united in their support for abstract ideals like freedom, equality and justice, but they have rarely agreed about what those ideals entail in concrete reality. Historians note that feminism has only ever commanded mass support when its political goals were compatible with many different beliefs and interests.

The movement for women's suffrage, which began in the nineteenth century and peaked in the early twentieth, is a case in point. Two of the central arguments deployed by campaigners rested on different – and theoretically incompatible – views about the nature and social role of women. One view emphasised women's similarity to men in order to argue that they deserved the same political rights, while the other emphasised women's difference from men, arguing that women's distinctive concerns could not be adequately represented by an all-male electorate. The movement's objective – gaining political representation for women – also brought together people whose other interests and allegiances were not just different, but in some cases directly opposed. For instance, in the US there were Black women whose support for the suffragist cause reflected the belief that women's enfranchisement would advance the struggle for racial justice; conversely, there were white feminists who courted southern segregationists by using the racist argument that enfranchising white women would bolster white supremacy. In Britain, where suffrage campaigners included supporters of the Conservative, Liberal and Radical parties,

Conservative women sometimes used the argument that women from the educated and propertied classes had a better claim to the vote than working-class men; socialists by contrast favoured enfranchising all women, as well as all men, since that would strengthen the position of the working class as a whole.

These disparate interest groups all stood to benefit from the extension of voting rights to women, and that was sufficient to bring them into an alliance; but given the depth of their other disagreements, it is not surprising that the alliance did not last. Once the vote had been won, women's differences reasserted themselves, and 'sex solidarity' gave way to conflict. In 1930s Britain, the division between feminists who emphasised women's similarity to men and those who emphasised women's distinctiveness produced two competing approaches which were labelled the 'old' and the 'new' feminism: the first campaigned for equality with men (for instance, equal pay and employment opportunities), while the other concentrated on improving women's situation as wives and mothers (for instance, through the provision of widows' pensions and family allowances).

This kind of pendulum swing has recurred in the history of feminism. The movement keeps being reinvented, partly to meet the challenges of new times, but also because of each new generation's desire to differentiate itself from the one before. This tendency is emphasised in one common way of organising historical narratives about feminism – through the idea that it has advanced in a series of 'waves'. According to this narrative, the 'first wave' began when women came together to demand legal and civil rights in the mid-nineteenth century, and ended with the victory of the suffrage campaign in the 1920s. The upsurge of feminist activism that began in the US (and quickly spread to other places) in the late 1960s was labelled 'the second wave' by activists who wanted to emphasise the continuity between their own movement and the more radical elements of nine-teenth-century feminism. A 'third wave' was proclaimed by a new generation of activists in the early 1990s, who explic-itly contrasted their approach with that of the second wave. The renewed interest in feminism that has become visible in the last ten years is sometimes described as a 'fourth wave'.

The 'wave' model, though widely used, has prompted numerous criticisms. One is that it oversimplifies history by implying that each new wave supersedes the previous one, when in fact the legacy of past waves remains visible in the present. Many second-wave creations (like women's studies courses and refuges for women escaping domestic violence) are still part of the contemporary feminist landscape, and there are some feminist organisations (like Britain's Fawcett Society, named after the suffragist Millicent Fawcett) whose approach would be recognisable to women of the first wave, supposing they were still around. The wave model has also been criticised for encouraging over-generalisations about the feminism of each historical moment – as though all the women who came of age politically in the 1960s, or in the 1990s, shared exactly the same beliefs and concerns. In reality they did not: political differences and disagreements (like the ones mentioned earlier within the suffrage move-ment) have existed in every wave, and among women of every generation. A third objection to the wave model is that its discontinuous narrative obscures the actual continuity of feminist activism, which didn't just stop in the 1920s and lie dormant until the late 1960s. The suffrage campaign ended when its objective was achieved, but campaigns to advance women's rights continued in other forms and other venues.

This points to a more general difficulty in writing the history of feminism as a political movement: it is, and always has been, decentralised and somewhat amorphous. Its history is not just the history of specifically feminist organisations (like the suffragist groups of the early twentieth century, or America's National Organization for Women, founded in the mid-1960s, or Britain's recently formed Women's Equality Party), but must also take account of all the other movements in which feminist goals have been pursued – for instance, the Labour movement, the co-operative movement, the peace movement and the environmentalist movement. Autonomous feminist politics – organised by women, for women – has often developed out of other political struggles, like the French Revolution in the late eighteenth century, the movement to abolish slavery in the nineteenth century, and the civil rights, anti-war and anti-colonialist movements of the twentieth century. Led by their involvement in these campaigns to see their own situation as oppressive, some women broke away to form their own, specifically feminist organisations. Others chose to stay where they were, but that does not mean they were not also feminists.

If we consider feminism in the third sense listed at the beginning of this introduction – as an intellectual framework – the picture is not much more straightforward. Feminism does not match our usual prototype for a philosophical movement or theoretical current (like, say, 'existentialism' or 'post-structuralism'), because it does not centre on the works of an agreed canon of Great Thinkers. There are some theoretical texts that are widely acknowledged as foundational in the history of modern feminist thought – like Mary Wollstonecraft's *A Vindication of the Rights of Woman* (1792) and Simone de Beauvoir's *The Second Sex* (1949) – but beyond that it would be hard to make a list that every feminist would agree on. 'Feminism' is a label that often comes with a pre-modifier, like 'Black', 'socialist', 'liberal', 'radical' or 'intersectional' (this is not an exhaustive list). Some of the categories overlap – an individual feminist can claim allegiance to several at once – while others are, or are seen as, opposed. On some issues there is relatively little disagreement among feminists, but on others the differences can be stark.

So far, then, my answer to the question 'What is feminism?' could be summed up in the formula 'It's complicated'. Feminism is multifaceted, diverse in both its historical forms and in its political and intellectual content: it's an umbrella, sheltering beliefs and interests that may be not just different but incompatible with one another. (And some of those beliefs are also held by people who deny they are feminists at all.) Is there anything that holds it all together, any set of basic principles to which all self-identified feminists subscribe? Many writers have concluded that the answer is 'no', and that we should speak not of 'feminism', singular, but of 'feminisms', plural. Attempts to universalise usually produce definitions that are too general to be helpful: for instance, 'feminism is an active desire to change women's position in society' immediately invites the question: 'change it from what to what?' (It might also invite the criticism that overtly anti-feminist groups also manifest 'an active desire to change women's position in society'.)

In this book I will aim to reflect and explore the complexity of feminism(s), but since we need to start from somewhere, I will start by offering a minimal definition which is slightly more informative than the very general one quoted above. Feminism undoubtedly comes in many different varieties, but all of them, arguably, rest on two fundamental beliefs:

1. That women currently occupy a subordinate position in society; that they suffer certain injustices and systemic disadvantages because they are women.
2. That the subordination of women is neither inevitable nor desirable: it can and should be changed through political action.

Feminists hold a range of views on the reasons why women occupy a subordinate position in society, how their subordination is maintained, who benefits from it and what its consequences are; but whatever their disagreements on these points, they all agree that women's subordination is real, and that it has existed in some form in the majority of human societies for which we have any record. Anti-feminists, by contrast, may dispute that women are subordinated: some supporters of the contemporary men's rights movement claim that women in modern Western societies have become the dominant sex. Other anti-feminist ideologies acknowledge the subordinate status of women, but justify it on the grounds that it is ordained by God and/or nature. Rejecting such justifications is another fundamental feminist principle. Though feminists may disagree on what changes they want to see in the position of women, all believe that change is necessary, and all assume that it is possible.

Although I have been using the generic term 'women', this account should not be taken to imply that 'women' form a single, internally homogeneous group who all suffer exactly the same injustices or disadvantages. Most currents of contemporary feminism incorporate the principle that Kimberlé Crenshaw labelled 'intersectionality', which acknowledges that women's experiences are shaped not only by their sex, but also by other aspects of their identity and social positioning, such as race, ethnicity, sexuality and social class. Different systems of dominance and subordination, such as sexism and racism, intersect to produce different outcomes for different groups of women, and not infrequently conflicts of interest between them. Though feminists believe that the subordinate status of women has negative consequences for all women, those consequences are not identical in every case.

The principle of intersectionality offers a way of thinking about the relationships among differently situated women within a single society. But we also have to think about the situations of women across national and regional boundaries: we live in a globalised world, and feminism today is a global movement. That point will be reflected in the following chapters, but in a book as short as this it is impossible to do justice to all of feminism's many regional and national forms. I should acknowledge, therefore, that my main focus will be on the Western (and more particularly, Anglo-American) feminism of the twentieth and twenty-first centuries. This is itself an internally diverse tradition (and one that has become increasingly aware of the need to think globally); but it is not the only one, and in making it my main reference point (a choice that reflects my own location) I am not suggesting that it is or should be the main reference point for all feminists everywhere.

The story of feminism is full of complications. The label 'feminist' has never been actively embraced by all women (or even the majority of women), and there have always been conflicts among the women who did embrace it. Yet feminism has survived: reports of its death always turn out to have been exaggerated. Its core idea – 'the radical notion that women are people' – is one that few people today would openly dissent from. But the devil is in the detail of what follows from that idea in practice. The answers feminists have given to that question are the subject of the rest of this book.

1

DOMINATION

Naomi Alderman's 2016 novel *The Power* imagines a future world where women are the dominant sex, and where it is generally assumed that they always have been. The main narrative purports to be the work of a male writer who wants to challenge this orthodoxy, by telling the story of a time in the distant past when women overthrew the rule of men. The revolution had begun when girls discovered that they could generate electricity in their own bodies, and use it to deliver painful or even fatal electric shocks. At first they used this power mainly in self-defence; but then they began to exploit it, and men's fear of it, for their own advantage. Soon women were running everything from national governments to organised crime. They became sexually aggressive, and sometimes abused men for their own pleasure. They created new myths that made their dominance appear natural; in time, the very idea that men had once had power would be dismissed as absurd, the product of idle speculation and wishful thinking.

Alderman has said of her book that it is only a dystopia if you're male: what happens to men in her imagined world is no worse than what women endure in the real one. But *The Power* doesn't fit the usual template for a feminist utopia either. The ideal societies of feminist speculative fiction – from Charlotte Perkins Gilman's *Herland* (1915) to Marge

Piercy's *Woman on the Edge of Time* (1976) – are generally egalitarian places where women live (either with or without men) in peace and harmony with nature. The world of *The Power* is more like our world, except that women and men have swapped places. The narrative invites us to ask whether women, if they had power over men, would abuse it in the same ways men have abused their power over women. But as we ponder this hypothetical question, we are bound to wonder why, in reality, women *don't* have power over men. Wherever one sex dominates the other, it is invariably men who dominate women. To us, this seems as self-evident as its opposite does in Alderman's fictional far-off future. Has there ever been a society in which women dominated men? Outside fiction and mythology, could such a society exist?

These questions have been debated, by feminists and others, for well over a century. In this chapter I consider some of the arguments writers have put forward about the origins of male dominance, how its forms have changed over time and what keeps it in place today. First, though, I should clarify what is – and what is not – meant by describing a society as 'male-dominated'.

General statements about male dominance are often met with the 'not all men' objection. Feminists are asked how they justify blaming men in general for things that only some men do, or are accused of glossing over the existence of women who do equally terrible things. So it's important to clarify that when feminists talk about male dominance, or 'patriarchy' (a term which literally means 'the rule of the father', but in feminist usage is more commonly a synonym for 'male dominance'), this is not a claim about the attitudes, intentions or behaviour of individual men. Rather, it's a claim about social structures. A male-dominated/patriarchal society is one whose structures and institutions – legal, political, religious, economic – put men in a position of power over women. Individual men may choose to forego certain rights and privileges, but that doesn't make men's collective structural dominance disappear. (Similarly, some capitalists treat their workers well, but that doesn't alter the fact that capitalism is a system based on inequality and exploitation.) When the philosopher John Stuart Mill married Harriet Taylor in 1851, he drew up a statement in which he promised that he would never make use of the rights the law gave husbands over their wives. But this promise had no legal standing: Mill was free to retract it at any time. His marriage could never be truly equal, because Taylor's position in it depended entirely on how he chose to treat her. Real equality is about structures, not the personal morality of individuals.

What does structural male dominance look like? The short answer is that it varies: it is neither uniform across cultures nor static and unchanging over time. However, if a society is male-dominated it will be likely to exhibit some or all of the following characteristics:

- Men monopolise or dominate positions of political power and leadership, and have more say in political decision-making than women.
- Men have rights under the law which women do not.
- Men own or control more economic resources than women.

- Men have direct authority – sanctioned by law, religion and custom – over women in their family or household.
- Men's activities, occupations, cultural products and ideas or forms of knowledge are accorded higher status than women's.
- Men use violence and the threat of it to control and intimidate women.

Different societies exhibit these characteristics in different ways and to differing degrees, and the profile of a single society may change significantly over time. Britain in John Stuart Mill's time was clearly male-dominated on every criterion. Today, British women are better (though still not equally) represented in politics, and their economic position has improved; they have the same legal rights as men, and men no longer have direct, legally sanctioned authority over their wives and daughters (though the prevalence of domestic violence, and in some communities 'honour' violence, shows that some men still feel entitled to assert their traditional prerogatives). Even within one society at one time, structural sex inequality will affect different groups of women differently. The general economic position of women in Britain may have improved since 1850, but the benefits have not been evenly distributed: there are clear differences between women of different generations, classes and ethnic groups, between more and less educated women, and between women who have children and those who don't.

Differences also exist among men, and that raises another question about what we mean by calling a society 'male dominated'. Do we mean that *all* men have more power, wealth, freedom and status than *all* women? The answer to that question is no. In societies which are stratified by caste, class or racial/ethnic divisions, many men will be excluded from political and economic power, and there will be women whose position in a higher social stratum gives them authority over men from a lower one. The slave-owner's wife could give orders to male slaves; the feudal lady of the manor had higher status than the male agricultural workers on her husband's estate. However, even the highest-ranking woman in feudal or plantation society was still required to submit to the authority of her husband. The same principle applied at other levels of the social hierarchy. The agricultural worker, for instance, was obliged to defer to his master's wife, but at home he could expect his own wife to defer to him.

The relevance of this point – essentially, that the same inequality between men and women is reproduced at every level of the social structure – is sometimes lost in discussions of the differences and inequalities among women. If a Hollywood megastar complains that her male co-star got paid twice as much as she did for their last film, some feminists will immediately suggest that she should check her privilege, pointing out that millions of women's lives would be transformed by even a tiny fraction of her enormous earnings. And of course, that is a legitimate point: I'm certainly not going to argue that fighting for gender parity among millionaires should be a feminist political priority. But it doesn't mean that the existence of a pay gap among Hollywood A-listers (or CEOs, or city bankers) is of no interest to feminists at all. It's another piece of evidence that male dominance is *structural*: it pervades the system from top to bottom. We may (indeed, we should) care more about its effects on women at the bottom, but what ultimately has to be dismantled is the whole edifice. This is why many feminists argue for retaining some general concept of male dominance, or patriarchy, while also recognising and paying attention to the differences among women.

But I still haven't answered the question I raised at the very beginning of this chapter: how common is male dominance itself? Is it found in all societies past and present, or have there been exceptions – societies where neither sex dominates, or where women dominate men? Many (though not all) feminists would say that egalitarian societies, where neither sex dominates, do exist, but female-dominated societies do not. There have, of course, been societies whose rulers were women, including some where a female despot or absolute monarch (like Catherine the Great of Russia) had enormous power over subjects of both sexes. However, a despotism in which the despot may be female is not the same thing as a structurally female-dominated society. Of the latter, the historical record provides no clear examples. Which raises the question: how do we explain their absence?

One traditional explanation relies on a form of biological determinism: male dominance is the inevitable consequence of the natural differences between the sexes. Men dominate women rather than vice versa (and by implication have always done so) because men are bigger, stronger and more aggressive, and because they are less constrained by their role in human reproduction. In its basic form, this argument is often presented as simple common sense, but it also comes in more elaborate, scientific versions. Evolutionary theorists have regularly argued that male dominance (or the traits which underpin it, like aggressiveness and competitiveness) evolved to serve the interest of both sexes in passing on their genes to offspring. Women, who must invest more time and energy in reproduction, can maximise their reproductive success by exchanging sex – and its products, children carrying both parents' genes – for men's services as providers and protectors. Their natural role is not to dominate, but to nurture.

This is not an argument favoured by most feminists, since it implies that male dominance and female subordination are inescapable facts of nature, whereas feminism requires the belief that our social arrangements can be changed. Commitment to that proposition has led many feminists (and other opponents of biological determinism, like Marxists) to ponder the historical origins of patriarchy. If patriarchy can be shown to have a history – if we can say when, where, how and for what reasons it originated – then we do not have to accept it as just part of the human condition: something was there before it, and something could be put in its place.

Reconstructing the origins of patriarchy is not a straightforward task, because the evidence (especially about the lives of our preliterate ancestors) is both limited and difficult to interpret. Nevertheless, various scholars have attempted it, drawing on the evidence provided by archaeology, anthropology, ancient history and the study of mythology. The earliest accounts were produced in the nineteenth century by men like the Swiss scholar Johann Jakob Bachofen and the American anthropologist Lewis Henry Morgan (who had spent time living among the Iroquois Indians). Both argued that patriarchy had displaced an earlier, matriarchal form of social organisation – 'matriarchal' in the literal sense of 'ruled by mothers'. Early human societies were imagined to have practised unregulated sexual promiscuity, or group marriage, which made it impossible to establish the paternity of children. These societies were therefore matrilineal (they traced descent through the female line), and the basic unit of society was the female-headed clan, centred on a group of sisters and their children. Patriarchy resulted from a shift to patrilineal descent. Under this system sisters were separated, each going to live with their husband's clan, to which their children would also belong.

On the question of why the shift occurred, perhaps the most influential early account was the one offered by Friedrich Engels in his 1884 book *The Origin of the Family, Private Property and the State*, which placed earlier scholarship within the framework of historical materialism, the Marxist approach which holds that 'the determining factor in history is … the production and reproduction of the immediate essentials of life'. Engels explained that this encompassed both 'the production of the means of existence, of articles of food and clothing, dwellings, and of the tools necessary for that production' and 'the production of human beings themselves, the propagation of the species'. In any given time and place, the overall organisation of society would reflect both the way in which labour was organised and the way that families were structured.

In Engels' account, the emergence of the patriarchal family followed from a change in 'the production of the means of existence', namely the development of pastoralism (the breeding and herding of domesticated animals). This increased the wealth of the clan, while also giving its men (who were generally responsible for tending livestock) a more important role. The men exploited their new position to ensure that they would be able to pass their property on to their own children. This required the replacement of the traditional system based on what Bachofen had dubbed 'mother-right' with one based on father-right. Engels famously described the imposition of this system as 'the world historical defeat of the female sex'. As a result of it, he wrote, 'the woman was degraded and reduced to servitude, she became the slave of [the man's] lust and a mere instrument for the production of children.'

In her 1986 book *The Creation of Patriarchy*, the historian Gerda Lerner presented a slightly different account. She agreed with Engels that the emergence of patriarchy was connected to new developments in the mode of production (farming), but disputed his argument that women were subjugated because of men's wish to secure the passage of their property to their own descendants. Rather, she argued that men turned women themselves, along with their children, *into* property. What motivated this was the increased demand for human labour which new modes of production created. In order to produce more children, communities needed more fertile women – a requirement which was often satisfied by capturing and enslaving women from neighbouring groups. 'Enslaved women and children', Lerner asserts, 'were the first property.'

Other feminists in the 1980s attempted to show that male dominance was not just the inevitable product of biological sex differences by focusing on present-day societies which were not organised on patriarchal principles. These societies, though sometimes labelled 'matriarchal', were not cases of female dominance; rather they were – or were said to be – gender-egalitarian. How far they really warranted that description was a subject of some debate among feminist anthropologists. Some argued that male dominance really is universal, pointing out that even in supposedly egalitarian societies it is men who dominate high-status public or ritual functions (for instance, among the matrilineal Iroquois, women are clan-mothers but only men serve as tribal chiefs). Others maintained that although there was usually a division of roles between men and women – they were not equal in the sense of 'identical and interchangeable' – their roles and the products of their labour were valued equally, and neither sex was exploited or controlled by the other.

Some of the clearest surviving cases of gender-egalitarianism are the hunter-gatherer societies which have maintained their traditional way of life. Studies suggest that men and women in these societies typically contribute equally to the survival of the community, play an equal part in decision-making and enjoy similar levels of personal and sexual freedom. In some cases there is little or no difference in their day-to-day activities (it is not true that women never hunt/fish, nor that men never gather). Hunter-gatherers are not just egalitarian in the negative sense of not having developed hierarchies: they actively cultivate an ethos of co-operation and sharing, and firmly discourage displays of individual dominance (individuals who flout this norm are subject to various community sanctions). Against the familiar argument that male dominance is a product of natural selection, some researchers have suggested that its absence may actually have been advantageous for the survival of our early human ancestors.

But while the existence of gender-egalitarian societies shows that male dominance is not a universal fact of nature, the examples described in the anthropological literature do not offer a very helpful model for feminists living in complex modern societies. It's true that they have inspired both fictional feminist utopias (Mattapoisett, for instance, the egalitarian society in Marge Piercy's novel *Woman on the Edge of Time*, is a technologically enhanced version of the culture of the matrilineal Wampanoag Indians) and some real-life experiments with alternative ways of living. But we can't all go back to foraging or horticulturalism, and few of us would want to. The goal of most feminists is to lessen, and ultimately eliminate, male dominance as it exists in the conditions of the twenty-first century. For that purpose it might be less important to probe the origins of patriarchy, and more important to analyse its current forms – which have clearly changed, not just since the dawn of civilisation, but since the 1880s when Engels was writing, and even since the feminist debates of the 1970s and 1980s.

In her book *Theorizing Patriarchy*, Sylvia Walby suggests that in societies like Britain during the last century there has been a gradual shift from 'private' to more 'public' forms of patriarchy. What she means by 'private' patriarchy is a system in which women are directly dominated by individual men – husbands, fathers, brothers – within the private sphere of the home and family. This was what male dominance looked like to Engels in the 1880s: the law gave men power over their wives, and for most women there was no alternative to becoming a wife, since they were barred from (or unqualified for) the kinds of paid work that would have enabled them to support themselves. Today this private form of male dominance has become less salient (though it cannot be said to have disappeared entirely). Most women in Britain now work outside the home; they can choose not to marry, or not to stay married, and they are no longer required by law to obey their husbands. That does not mean, however, that they are no longer subordinated in any way. Rather, it means that they experience their subordinate status less in their private relationships with individual men, and more in their public roles as citizens and employees.

In the sphere of work, for instance (discussed further in chapter 3), women are concentrated in low-paid and low-status occupations, they are subject to sex discrimination, and they are disadvantaged by the expectation that they will also be responsible for unpaid care work at home. In recent decades, 'austerity' programmes scaling back public service provision have had a particularly negative effect on women, both because the services in question are major employers of women, and because the withdrawal of public services increases the amount of unpaid care work women have to do.

Sex is another domain in which Walby suggests there has been a shift in the form that male dominance typically takes. The last 50 years are often thought of as an era of sexual liberation: if we compare the situation in Britain today with the one that prevailed in the 1960s, we see that sexual minorities have gained greater social acceptance, and the stigma attached to heterosexual sex outside marriage has decreased. The risk of unwanted pregnancy has been reduced by access to reliable contraception, and it is no longer assumed that 'normal' women are uninterested in sex. But while in many ways these developments have been positive for both sexes, feminists have criticised the idea that women now have the same sexual freedom as men. Here too, arguably, there has been a shift from private patriarchy – a system in which women are defined as the exclusive sexual property of their husbands – to a more public form in which it is assumed that women are or should be sexually available to any man. What used to be forbidden to women and girls is now expected of them, and all too often it is forced on them. This form of male dominance, whether manifested in the phenomenon of sexual bullying in schools, 'rape culture' on college campuses, sexual harassment at work or presidential boasts about 'grabbing [women] by the pussy', is central to the maintenance of modern patriarchal power, and as such has become an increasingly visible focus for feminist political activism.

As we saw earlier, virtually all accounts of the origins of patriarchy suggest that a significant factor in its emergence was the desire of men to exploit and control women's reproductive capacities. Some feminists have argued that women were unable to resist male dominance precisely because they were, to quote Shulamith Firestone, 'at the continual mercy of their biology'. But by the time Firestone was writing (in 1970), advances in science and technology had changed this. She even suggested that in future artificial reproduction could be used to free women from their biological burden entirely. This proposal was never widely accepted among feminists, but most were in agreement with Firestone's demand for 'the full restoration to women of ownership over their own bodies'. The liberation of women could not be achieved unless women themselves, rather than men and male-dominated institutions (the state, the church, the medical profession), decided whether and when they would bear children.

In the US in 1970, one key political battle in this area was for the right to legal abortion (Roe v. Wade, the Supreme Court case which ultimately established that right, was still three years away). In Britain, where abortion had been decriminalised in 1967, but only on condition that a woman's need for it was certified by two doctors, feminists campaigned for it to be available on demand. The activists involved in these campaigns expected that in time their goals would be achieved. But nearly 50 years later, progress has stalled almost everywhere. New restrictions on abortion have multiplied; in some places (such as Poland) there have been attempts to outlaw it entirely, and in some US states laws have been proposed that effectively give fathers a right of veto.

This renewed enthusiasm for one of the oldest of all patriarchal practices – forcing women to bear children

– points to a wider problem confronting feminism in the twenty-first century: the rise of new and militant patriarchal movements, including both modern forms of religious fundamentalism and secular men's rights groups (which often have links to racist and nationalist organisations: white supremacy, male supremacy and hatred of Muslims and Jews are the main causes of the so-called alt-right). The once-marginal ideologies of these movements have now gained not only influence, but real political power. An obvious case in point is the current US administration, in which (as I write in 2017) a Christian fundamentalist serves as vice president. But this isn't just a 'first-world problem'. Some religious fundamentalist groups in Africa and the Middle East, like Boko Haram and ISIS, have adopted, in the course of their various insurgencies, the ancient patriarchal practice of capturing, raping and enslaving women and girls. Women's bodily autonomy, both sexual and reproductive, is threatened in both old and new ways, and resisting that threat is therefore high on feminism's current agenda.

Male dominance is not just something that is imposed on women against their will: women themselves have often accepted, or been complicit in, their own subordination. Women as well as men support leaders, and vote for governments, who make no secret of their determination to curtail women's rights. Women as well as men are active in social and religious movements that champion traditional (i.e. patriarchal) 'family values'. Why women so often act against what might appear to be their own interests is a question feminists have often asked, and two kinds of answers have been offered frequently.

One answer focuses on the nature of women's relationship with men. Masters may try to win the affections of their servants, slaves, imperial subjects, tenants or workers (and they may sometimes succeed), but there is no other form of structural inequality which calls for members of the subordinated group to form a lifelong bond of the most intimate kind with a member of the dominant group. Even when women are not dependent on men for protection and subsistence, their love for their husbands, brothers and sons encourages identification with their interests ('what's good for my family is good for me'). In addition, the patriarchal family in its modern, nuclear form tends to separate women from one another, making it harder for them to develop the kind of collective solidarity that is needed for effective resistance to oppression.

The other answer focuses on the way girls and women are socialised to accept their subordinate position as natural, inevitable and just. One important agent of this socialisation is the family, but others include religion (virtually all the world's major religions have traditionally taught that the subordination of women to men is divinely ordained) and education, or the lack of it. As Gerda Lerner notes, for most of human history almost all women were excluded from advanced learning and so played little part in the creation of knowledge. That too has changed in recent times; but it will take more than a few decades to undo the effects of thousands of years of male dominance on the way people of both sexes understand the world. The pre-eminent form of contemporary knowledge, science, continues to be dominated by men: today it could be argued that scientific accounts of male-female differences contribute as much to the maintenance of patriarchy as do traditional religious ones. On the other hand, science – like religion before it – can offer women a base from which to challenge male dominance and male-centred knowledge.

It is often argued that both sexes are oppressed by the social arrangements which are characteristic of patriarchal societies. Men may be the dominant sex, but the norms of masculinity subject them to demands and expectations (e.g. that they will suppress their emotions and never show weakness, work long hours to support their families, and fight wars on behalf of their countries) which many experience as a burden rather than a privilege. But while most feminists would agree that individual men pay a price for the dominant position they occupy as a class, they would also point out that men benefit from this arrangement in ways that women do not. For that reason, many feminists reject what Susan Sontag once called 'the cliché that when women are liberated men will be liberated too'. As Sontag says, the idea that patriarchy oppresses everyone equally 'slides over the raw reality of male domination – as if this were an arrangement in fact arranged by nobody, which suits nobody, which works to nobody's advantage'. Male dominance persists for the same reason any other system of structural inequality persists: because it does work to somebody's advantage. What feminists hope is that understanding how it works will help us take the actions needed to change it.

2

RIGHTS

Mainstream reference sources agree: feminism is about 'women's rights'. The Oxford Dictionary defines it as 'the advocacy of women's rights on the ground of the equality of the sexes'. The New World Encyclopedia says that it 'comprises a number of social, cultural and political movements … concerned with gender inequalities and equal rights for women'. Any search for feminist quotations will also turn up references to women's rights, from 'men, their rights and nothing more; women, their rights and nothing less' (the motto of *The Revolution*, a newspaper founded in 1868 by the American suffragists Susan B. Anthony and Elizabeth Cady Stanton), to 'women's rights are human rights' (a formula first used in 1990 by Charlotte Bunch, and popularised in a speech made five years later by Hillary Clinton). Not all feminists would endorse this mainstream definition. Demands for rights belong to a liberal political tradition; many feminists would argue that the ultimate goal, ending women's oppression, cannot be achieved without more radical social change. From this perspective, defining feminism as a movement for 'women's rights' does not do justice to the breadth of its ambitions. Nevertheless, it is fair to say that the concept of rights has played an important part in feminist politics – both the theory and the practice – throughout the movement's history.

This history begins in the eighteenth century, when philosophical ideas about 'the rights of man' were being taken up and acted on by revolutionary political movements. In the famous words of the American Declaration of Independence, written in 1776 by Thomas Jefferson:

> We hold these truths to be self-evident, that all men are created equal, that they are endowed by their Creator with certain unalienable rights, that among these are Life, Liberty and the Pursuit of Happiness.

The rights being proclaimed here are what theorists call 'natural rights', rights that belong to human beings by virtue of their nature (the modern concept of 'human rights' expresses a similar idea). But when Jefferson wrote 'all men', he did not mean 'all human beings'. The 'men' whose rights the Declaration asserted were specifically white and male: they did not include slaves, or the indigenous people of North America, and they did not include women of any race. Nor were women included in 1789 when revolutionaries in France issued a Declaration of the Rights of Man and of the Citizen. But this omission did not go unopposed. In 1791 the playwright Olympe de Gouges published her own Declaration of the Rights of Woman and of the Female Citizen (one of the offences for which she was sent to the guillotine two years later). And in England around the same time, another keen observer of events in France – Mary Wollstonecraft – produced *A Vindication of the Rights of Woman.*

A Vindication argued that there was no legitimate basis for excluding women from 'the rights of man'. For thinkers of this time, the defining quality of 'man', from which his natural rights derived, was the ability to reason: it was reason which, as Wollstonecraft put it, 'raises men above the brute creation'. And by 'men' she did mean 'all human beings'. She took issue with the argument that was used to justify withholding rights from women, that they lacked men's capacity for rational thought. Most women, she agreed, had not developed their powers of reason to the same level as most men, but in her view that was a matter of nurture rather than nature, the result of women's inferior education. 'Taught from infancy that beauty is woman's sceptre', she wrote, 'the mind shapes itself to the body, and roaming round its gilt cage, only seeks to adorn its prison.' Women were, nevertheless, rational creatures just as men were, and as such they too were endowed with natural rights.

A Vindication was more a philosophical treatise than a political manifesto. But in the second half of the nineteenth century, feminists of what we now call the 'first wave' would build on the general argument for women's rights with organised campaigns for specific legal and civil rights. The rights these feminists demanded included women's right to be educated, to earn a living, to enter professions that had previously been closed to them, to own property (rather than ceding it to their husbands when they married), to divorce their husbands, and to participate alongside men in political decision-making. This tradition has shaped the popular understanding of feminism as a movement for women's rights – and also the idea that 'women's rights' means 'equal rights', since the goal of many early campaigns was to secure for women rights that men already had.

Today, in many parts of the world, this liberal, equal rights version of feminism has become mainstream common sense. It seems self-evident that women and men should be equal before the law, and only fair that they should have the same rights and opportunities in spheres like education, work and politics. It is easy to forget how recently this became a matter of consensus. As a child in Britain in the 1960s, I was surrounded by adult women who had grown up without what we would now consider basic rights. When my grandmother came of age in the 1920s, women under 30 were still not allowed to vote. When my mother got married in the 1950s, she could not apply for a loan without my father's permission. When I left school in 1976, workplace sex discrimination had only just been made illegal (and the first few employers I worked for evidently hadn't got the memo). Thinking about what has changed for women in my own country during my own lifetime is a salutary reminder of what campaigns for rights have achieved. At the same time, when I think about what hasn't changed, it's clear that the rights approach has limitations.

Some feminists have always rejected equal rights as a 'reformist' goal, one which aims to improve women's position in society without radically changing society itself. The American anarchist and feminist Emma Goldman refused to support campaigns for women's suffrage, saying that 'activists ought to advocate revolution rather than seek greater privileges within an inherently unjust system'. In 1969, nearly 50 years after the vote had been won in the US, radical feminists held a protest in which they symbolically handed it back: voting, they maintained, had done nothing to liberate women from oppression.

Other feminists, however, have defended demands for rights against the criticism that they are insufficiently radical. The legal theorist Nicola Lacey observes that some of the strongest arguments on this point have come from Black and indigenous feminists, or those located in the global South, who see feminist critiques of rights as reflecting the perspective of the relatively privileged – white women in Western liberal democracies where basic rights are already well-established. 'For the more deeply oppressed', writes Lacey, 'the language of rights still represents an aspiration and ideal; it can only be deconstructed once a prior political battle has been won.' In places where that battle is still ongoing (like Saudi Arabia, where women recently won the right to hold driving licences, but still cannot marry, travel or sign contracts without the permission of a male guardian), activists do not regard campaigns for rights as irrelevant: they are well aware that other things (in particular, cultural norms and attitudes) will have to change if women are to be equal citizens in practice, but establishing rights in principle and in law is still a key objective.

One thing that just about everyone agrees on is that decades of campaigns, initiatives and legislation promoting equal rights around the world have not actually delivered equality. Even where the evidence suggests that women's position is improving, their progress appears painfully slow. The much-discussed gender pay gap, for instance, is smaller than it once was, but in 2015 the World Economic Forum predicted that it would not actually close until 2133. Why are goals like equal pay, which command widespread support in theory, so difficult to achieve in practice?

One problem that feminists have identified is the tendency for laws to be based on a principle of equal treatment, something which implicitly requires women to be the same as men in order to be treated 'equally'. For instance, equal pay legislation typically provides a legal remedy for women who can show they are being paid less than men for doing the same work. What this does not address, however, is the pervasive sex segregation of many labour markets. Large numbers of women earn low wages precisely because they do *not* do the same work as men: they work in traditionally female occupations, or in female-dominated enclaves within a sector that also employs men. Paradoxically, then, the women who are most disadvantaged by the undervaluing of women's work are also the ones who gain least from a formal right to equal pay.

Another issue on which progress has been slow is the under-representation of women in political assemblies. The United Nations has a target of 30 per cent for women's representation in national legislatures: in 2011 fewer than 30 countries had met it. In some places this has been addressed by setting quotas to ensure that a certain number of women will be elected. This approach recognises that female and male candidates are not competing on the proverbial level playing field: women are disadvantaged by an implicit bias in men's favour. Measures like quota-setting are meant to compensate for that bias. But they frequently provoke resistance on the grounds that they are biased themselves:

they violate the basic principle of equal rights by not treating men and women identically.

Some rights of particular importance to women cannot easily be justified on the basis that all individuals should be treated the same, because they relate to women's role in reproduction. In both the US and the UK, discrimination against pregnant women was not initially seen as a clear case of sex discrimination (though it is now recognised as such in both jurisdictions). Employers could and did argue that their problem wasn't with women as such, but only with those who had decided to become pregnant – and the women this affected couldn't claim that they were being treated less favourably than men in the same position would be, since there were no men in the same position.

Another right relating to reproduction is the right to terminate a pregnancy legally. The long and continuing struggle over abortion raises another pertinent question about the equal rights approach: what happens when women's rights are, or are seen to be, in conflict with other rights? In jurisdictions that prohibit abortion, the justification is usually that allowing it would violate the unborn child's right to life. Abortion may be permitted where the mother's own life is threatened, but only her right to life, not her right to bodily autonomy, can take priority over the rights of the foetus. Another argument which is sometimes used is that mothers should not have rights which fathers are denied. Laws like those mentioned in chapter 2, which give fathers the right to prevent mothers from terminating a pregnancy, invoke the 'equal treatment without regard to sex' principle, but on the basis (feminists would argue) of a false equivalency – it may take two to conceive a child, but only one can gestate and give birth to it. Such provisions treat a father's rights over his child as more important than a mother's rights over her own body.

Abortion is not the only area where conflicting rights may be an issue. The rights of women may also be in tension with general rights such as the right to privacy, to family life and to the expression of cultural or religious beliefs. This tension reflects the historical origins of the rights framework, which was essentially designed to regulate men's dealings with the government and one another in the public sphere of politics and commerce. It did not reach into the private sphere to regulate men's relationships with other members of their own households – the women, children, servants and slaves who under the original 'social contract' had no rights of their own. Rather, private life was seen as an area where men should be free from outside interference.

The traces of this idea can still be seen in the text which inaugurated the modern era of 'human rights', the Universal Declaration of Human Rights (UDHR) adopted by the UN General Assembly in 1948. Unlike its eighteenth-century ancestors, the Declaration explicitly recognises 'the equal rights of men and women' in its Preamble. But in Article 16 it also says that 'the family is the natural and fundamental group unit of society and is entitled to protection by society and the State' – an assertion which fails to acknowledge that the family is not an internally homogeneous unit, and that the interests of its members may not always coincide. As feminists have been pointing out for decades, a very high proportion of the abuse suffered by women and girls, from forced labour to domestic and sexual violence, is inflicted on them within the family, by other family members. There is, therefore, a potential contradiction between the state's duty to protect the family, and its duty to protect 'the equal rights of men and women'.

This contradiction is illustrated in many states' responses to CEDAW, the Convention on the Elimination of All Forms of Discrimination Against Women, which the UN adopted in 1979. This represented a more concerted effort to address the issue of women's rights: unlike the UDHR, which does not have the force of a treaty, UN Conventions impose concrete obligations on those member states that ratify them. However, states are not obliged to sign up to every UN Convention (the US, for instance, chose not to ratify CEDAW), and they also have the option of ratifying a Convention while entering reservations – identifying specific obligations that they are not willing to be bound by. In the case of CEDAW, the list of these reservations was very lengthy, and many of them related to provisions dealing with women's position in the family. Several countries could not accept that married women should have the right to choose their own domicile, or their own name, and many insisted that only fathers could pass their nationality on to their children. Malta reserved the right to treat a married woman's income as her husband's for tax purposes, and to pay him, as the 'head of household', state benefits due to her. Britain (along with Lesotho) wanted to ensure that first-born sons would continue to inherit the Crown. A number of majority Muslim states (including Bahrain, Egypt, Saudi Arabia, Malaysia, the Maldives, Mauretania and Morocco) declared that they would not be bound by any provision that conflicted with Islamic law: many expressed specific concerns about the provisions on marriage and divorce, where (in the words of Morocco's reservation), 'equality ... is considered incompatible with the Islamic Shariah, which guarantees to each of the spouses rights and responsibilities within a framework of equilibrium and complementarity.'

These reservations illustrate the difficulty of developing an international framework for women's rights. As the legal theorist Catharine MacKinnon has pointed out, gender inequality is a global system, but attempts to address it as such can be frustrated in two ways. If a form of inequality or oppression is culturally specific, the state(s) concerned can object to the imposition of 'alien' cultural norms. This is how so many states were able to ratify a Convention whose stated purpose was 'the elimination of all forms of discrimination against women', while reserving the right to continue discriminating on such consequential matters as marriage, divorce, inheritance and nationality. But if a form of gender inequality or oppression is culturally widespread or universal, that may license the argument that it is 'only natural', and that the state can do nothing about it.

This is why the slogan 'women's rights are human rights' is not just, as it might first appear, a tautology ('women are human, therefore their rights are human rights'). It was intended as a reproach to the international human rights movement for its failure to take women's rights, and more especially abuses of their rights, seriously. In 1990, Charlotte Bunch, the US feminist who is widely credited with introducing the slogan (though Bunch herself has said that she first heard it used by women activists in the Philippines), gave a blunt summary of what the attitudes mentioned above ('it's a cultural matter', or 'it's only natural') were excusing. Women around the world, she noted, 'are routinely subject to torture, starvation, terrorism, humiliation, mutilation, and even murder simply because they are female'. If these practices targeted some other group, they would surely be seen as obvious human rights violations; but in the case of women that was not how they were seen.

In 1991 activists started a petition calling on the next UN World Conference on Human Rights, which was to be held in 1993 in Vienna, to recognise that 'violence against women violates human rights'. By the time the petition was presented at the conference, it had been signed by half a million people, and sponsored by a thousand organisations in 124 countries. Later in the year the UN formally adopted a Declaration on the Elimination of Violence Against Women, and the issue has continued to move up its agenda. In 1998 references to gender-based persecution and sexual violence were included in the statute that founded the International Criminal Court; in 2000 the UN adopted a resolution on violence against women in the context of armed conflict (some might say belatedly, given that a series of conflicts during the 1990s – in former Yugoslavia, Rwanda and the Democratic Republic of Congo – had brought the use of mass rape as a weapon of war and genocide to worldwide attention).

Meanwhile, in 1995, the 4th UN World Conference on Women in Beijing (the event where Hillary Clinton used the words 'women's rights are human rights'), produced the

'Beijing Platform for Action' and the associated approach of 'gender mainstreaming'. Rather than treating women's rights as a separate issue, the UN now integrates a gender perspective into all its work. For any policy or programme it plans to adopt, it asks what the impact on women will be: will their position be affected positively, negatively or not at all? The same approach is used in monitoring and evaluating policies after they are implemented. The aim is to promote gender equality and, conversely, to avoid perpetuating inequality. In 2010, the UN created an 'Entity for Gender Equality and the Empowerment of Women', more commonly known as 'UN Women', which supports both UN policymakers and the efforts of member states to implement international standards.

I've focused on the UN here because its policies and standards are so widely influential – not only for the governments of member states, but also for non-governmental organisations (NGOs) around the world. The developments just described in its approach to women's rights since 1990 have had a significant impact, especially in making opposition to violence against women a higher priority. But the question of how women's rights are defined and understood remains a complex and challenging one, especially for a movement that aspires to be global, intersectional and inclusive.

The documents I have mentioned or quoted in this chapter typically treat 'women' as an undifferentiated category, defined by the simple contrast with 'men'. But in reality, of course, 'women' are not undifferentiated: their situations and their needs are shaped by differences of age, class, race, ethnicity, sexuality, religious belief or non-belief, marital status, maternal status, rural versus urban location, and location in the global South versus the North. Just as there may be conflicts between the rights of women and those of men, or children, so there may also be conflicts between different groups of women. To illustrate this, let us briefly consider two current issues on which women, and feminists, are divided.

The first issue is commercial surrogacy – an arrangement where a person or couple commissions and pays a woman to gestate and give birth to a child for them (the embryo implanted into the 'gestational surrogate' may be created using genetic material from either the prospective parents or from donors). This has become a transnational form of commerce, partly for reasons of cost (it follows the same logic that has led to 'offshoring' in other industries), and also because commercial surrogacy is prohibited in many European countries, including Britain. European clients can, however, approach clinics in countries outside Europe, which recruit women to act as surrogates, oversee the necessary medical procedures and in some cases run hostels where women are monitored during pregnancy.

This trade has prompted debate about the rights of both the surrogates and the clients. Although feminists generally support reproductive choice, which includes the right to have children as well as the right not to, opponents of commercial surrogacy maintain that there is no right to exploit another woman for that purpose. Where the surrogates are women from poor communities in the global South, campaigners argue that the transaction is unavoidably exploitative, and puts the women involved at risk of abuse (for instance, of being coerced into surrogacy by families desperate for money, or subjected to treatments whose long-term effects they are not fully informed of). Other feminists, however, see these arguments as denying women agency and choice. If feminists believe in women's right to bodily autonomy, that surely means that poor women in South and South East Asia have a right to sell their services as gestational surrogates (similar arguments are made about the sale of sexual services, a question I will come back to in chapter 5). For feminists who take this view, there is no conflict between the rights of the client and those of the surrogate, and outlawing surrogacy would unfairly restrict the rights of both.

But it could be asked whether the problem commercial surrogacy raises is really about rights at all. We often talk about 'rights', not to mention 'agency' and 'choice', as if they were exercised in a vacuum, when in reality what we do is both enabled and constrained by the conditions in which we have to operate. In this case, for instance, we are dealing with choices which no one could have made before the advent of new reproductive technologies. Individual women's choices are also shaped by the extreme economic inequality which makes this business model viable (affordable for overseas clients, economically worthwhile for local surrogates, and profitable for the clinics). If women in places like rural Gujarat had more and better economic options, how many would choose to be gestational surrogates for wealthy foreigners? In Britain in the nineteenth century it could have been said that millions of women 'chose' to enter domestic service – but when other options became available during and after the First World War the supply of live-in servants diminished rapidly.

Another question on which feminists are divided concerns the cultural and religious rights of minority women. In Europe there is particular controversy about the public wearing of religious symbols, especially the niqab or face veil worn by some Muslim women, which is now prohibited in France and Belgium. There has also been some debate about the role played by religious courts in arbitrating marital and family disputes, and the differential treatment of boys and girls in some faith schools. The context in which these matters are debated is one of rising anti-Muslim racism. Many feminists, along with leftists and liberals more generally, understand measures like the banning of the niqab as a form of discrimination motivated primarily by racism, and are incensed when the authorities responsible claim to be motivated by feminist concerns about the rights of Muslim women. In addition to denouncing these claims as cynical, some feminists have condemned them for presenting Muslim women as helpless victims who need to be 'rescued' by Western liberals. Many Muslim women have objected both to the assumption that they have not made their own choices, and to the idea that non-Muslim feminists should debate what is oppressive to Muslim women rather than taking their cue from what those women say themselves.

Undoubtedly it is important to listen to what Muslim women say. But political arguments are rarely settled by these calls to 'listen to what the women from group X say', because listening to the women from group X will soon reveal that they are not all saying the same thing. The fact that women share an identity does not guarantee that they will share the same political analysis. There are Muslim feminists who campaign in support of religious rights; there are also Muslim feminists who take the opposite view.

Marième Hélie-Lucas, an Algerian feminist living in France, has defended the French ban on veiling in schools, arguing that the state has a responsibility to protect children from damaging practices imposed on them by their parents. Liberals and leftists, she says, have too often been willing to abdicate that responsibility in relation to girls from minority ethnic groups: in the past, some on the Left defended practices like FGM (female genital mutilation) as a 'cultural right', and denounced efforts to eradicate it in Europe as 'Western imperialism'. She also observes that these accusations of 'Western imperialism' display a rather Eurocentric ignorance of the activities and writings of non-Western feminists. Grassroots movements to eliminate FGM have existed in Africa for decades, and there is a tradition of Islamic feminism which has argued since the nineteenth century that while the Qur'an requires modesty (in both sexes), veiling as such is a cultural imposition. (Of course, not all African or Middle Eastern feminists agree with these positions: there are differences and disagreements among feminists everywhere.)

The British Muslim feminist Yasmin Rehman, while acknowledging that women may veil by choice, warns against assuming that it is always an exercise of their individual agency. Long before the niqab became a matter of public controversy, South Asian women in Britain were speaking out about being forced to wear other traditional garments, like the shalwar kameez (a loose tunic and trousers), and more generally about the way community norms of 'modest' dress (which also exist in non-Muslim communities) were used to control women and girls. Rehman acknowledges the difficulty, in present conditions, of criticising minority cultural practices without fanning the flames of racism, but she argues that feminists should support minority women and girls who are challenging a community's sexist norms from the inside, just as they support women and girls who resist sexism within the majority community.

Southall Black Sisters (SBS), a British feminist group with a long record of campaigning for the rights of Black and South Asian women, has become increasingly concerned about the growing official acceptance of religious courts as arbiters of disputes about marriage, divorce, child custody, inheritance and domestic violence. In 2016, 300 women signed a statement supporting SBS's 'one law for all' campaign:

> We know from personal experiences that many religious bodies such as Sharia Councils are presided over by hard-line or fundamentalist clerics who are intolerant of the very idea that women should be in control of their own bodies and minds. These clerics ... abuse their positions of power by shaming and slandering those of us who reject those aspects of our religions and cultures that we find oppressive. We pay a huge price for not submitting to domestic violence, rape, polygamy and child abuse.

SBS frames this campaign as a defence of minority women's right to equal citizenship. The problem is not only that religious courts treat women and men unequally, but also that the acceptance of these courts alongside secular ones creates inequality between minority women and others. It allows women's status as minority community members to take precedence over their status as citizens of the UK, and leaves their rights to be adjudicated by a parallel justice system whose workings are neither transparent nor democratically accountable (Parliament can change the law of the land, but not the law of God).

Other feminists, however, have made the opposite argument – that insisting on 'one law for all' effectively denies some minority women the same access to justice as other citizens. There are things women with certain beliefs may need (e.g. a religiously valid divorce which leaves them free to remarry) which they cannot get from a secular court. Once again, the underlying question here is about the balance between sameness and difference: does equality require that everyone be treated the same, or can some kinds of equality only be achieved by *not* treating everyone identically?

'Rights' and 'equality' are familiar, mainstream concepts, but they are not always as simple as they appear. And while rights do have an important place in feminism, both historically and in the present, they are only one part of the bigger picture. Without other kinds of change – social, cultural and economic – the rights women possess on paper may do little, in practice, to improve their lives.

3

WORK

What would you expect to find in a chapter about feminist perspectives on work? I'm guessing that popular answers might include the gender pay gap, the under-representation of women in certain industries, the 'glass ceiling', and the problem of what's often called the 'work-life balance'. These are all subjects which feature prominently in media coverage of 'women's issues': the attention they receive both reflects and reinforces the popular belief that getting women into the workplace – and especially into high-status careers – is one of the main goals, if not *the* main goal, of feminism. That assumption has prompted conservatives to complain that feminism devalues women's traditional role in the home, while radicals complain that it focuses too narrowly on the 'first-world problems' of elite professional women. Both criticisms, however, could be said to attack a 'straw feminism'. Feminist ideas about work are both more varied and more complicated than the popular stereotype acknowledges.

Popular discussions of women and work often equate 'work' specifically with *paid* work – labour that is exchanged for money, in the form of wages, fees or a salary. Our everyday ways of talking make the same equation. For instance, people ask new mothers whether they plan to go 'back to work', as if looking after a baby were not 'work'. One of the defining features of a feminist perspective is the recognition that caring for a family is also work: the difference is that you don't get paid to do it. And that is a feminist issue, because most unpaid care work is done by women. This fact is often invoked as a common-sense explanation for things like the gender pay gap ('women earn less than men because they have family responsibilities'). But for feminists it isn't good enough to treat women's 'family responsibilities' as self-evident: we need to explain why only women are required to perform this balancing act, and why it is seen as a problem for individual women to solve rather than an issue for society as a whole.

Another problem with the familiar list of 'women and work' issues is that many of them can easily be dismissed as the concerns of a small and highly privileged minority. Most women around the world don't have the luxury of worrying about career choices and glass ceilings: they work to pay the rent and put food on the table. It's not just that elite professional women are in a different situation from less privileged women: their high-powered careers may actually depend on those women's labour as cleaners, housekeepers, nannies and babysitters. These jobs are done predominantly by working-class women, women of colour, and – increasingly – migrant women from poorer parts of the world. Their situation (working, and sometimes also living, in their employer's home) is one that can leave them vulnerable to exploitation and abuse. Charities have documented many cases where the conditions of work amount to slavery, with workers forbidden to leave the house, forced to work without wages, deprived of their passports and subjected to physical and sexual violence.

Feminism does have to consider the situation of all women, not just some; it must be able to deal with differences and inequalities between women, and with the exploitation of some by others. But as I noted in the introduction, one of feminism's core beliefs is that women are oppressed *as women*. So a feminist analysis must also ask how relationships among women (including unequal or exploitative ones) are affected by the fact that they are women rather than men.

For instance, we might ask why the exploitation of poor women's domestic labour is so often presented as the exclusive responsibility of wealthier women. From a feminist perspective, there's another party to this transaction, even if he remains discreetly in the background: the man of the household. This particular form of exploitation is shaped by the expectation that a wife is responsible for taking care of the house and the children; if she doesn't want to provide those services herself, it's her responsibility to find a substitute. Her husband benefits from this arrangement as much as she does (without it he would either have to share the work or accept a lower standard of service). But he is not seen as the exploiter, because he hasn't chosen to pay someone else to do 'his' job.

You might say: but surely that's the point – the wife in a wealthy household isn't going out to work because she has to, but because she wants to. She *is* making a choice, and it's a choice most women don't have. Many women would envy her freedom not to work outside the home. But this overlooks another point. A full-time housewife – regardless of her social class – is financially dependent on her husband,

and that dependence is a form of inequality that not only disadvantages her in their relationship (without an income she will find it hard to escape if he abuses her, for instance), it also contributes to the economic disadvantage women collectively suffer. The idea that women can depend on the income of a male 'breadwinner' has persistently been used to justify paying all women lower wages, and that exacerbates the poverty of many households which do, in fact, depend on women's earnings. These are all reasons why feminists since the nineteenth century have seen access to paid work as an important political demand. And it isn't just important for the most privileged Western women.

In 1990, the economist Amartya Sen wrote an article entitled 'More than 100 million women are missing'. He based this claim on an analysis of population statistics showing that in certain parts of the world, like North Africa and much of Asia, men are significantly more numerous than women. In China in the 1980s the ratio was 94 women for every 100 men. In the Indian state of Punjab it was 86 women to 100 men. These figures are striking because they reverse the expected pattern. More boys than girls are born (the normal ratio is about 105 to 100), but because infant mortality is higher among boys and, at the other end of the age spectrum, life expectancy is greater for women, the norm – other things being equal – is for the overall population to contain a slightly higher percentage of women. Exceptions arise when other things are not equal: when girls and women are not valued, or treated, equally, and the result is disproportionately high rates of female mortality. Girls and women die because they are not given enough to eat, or because they do not receive the medical care they need. In some cases, infant girls are deliberately neglected or even killed. And today, we know that many girls are never born, because families use sex-selective abortion to avoid having daughters.

Sen does not think that this is just a matter of women losing out to men where economic resources are scarce. He notes that men do not outnumber women in most of sub-Saharan Africa, a region which contains some of the world's poorest countries; in India, too, the imbalance is greater in Punjab, a relatively wealthy state, than in Kerala, a much poorer one. The real issue, he argues, is how resources are distributed within households. And this, he believes, can be related to the question of women's work: in particular, whether women engage in productive labour that makes a tangible contribution to the household economy. His analysis suggests that women are valued more, and treated better, when they are 'gainfully employed', earning money outside the household.

Women who are not 'gainfully employed' are nevertheless, as Sen recognises, working. Typically, they are spending many hours each day on activities like cooking, cleaning, laundering and mending clothes, caring for children, the old and the sick. In some of the societies he discusses they may also be undertaking such time-consuming household tasks as collecting water and gathering firewood. But this work is, as he puts it, 'unpaid and unhonoured'. Its real economic contribution goes unrecognised, because its products are largely intangible (housework is classed by many theorists as 'reproductive' rather than productive work: it enables other members of the household to engage in productive labour by freeing them from tasks like food preparation which they would otherwise have to do for themselves). And this is not just an issue for women in North Africa or Punjab. Reproductive work has to be done in every society, and in every society that has consequences for women.

In 2014, the Organisation for Economic Co-operation and Development (OECD) reported that 'around the world, women spend two to ten times more time on unpaid care work than men'. As this wording implies, there are differences between regions and countries (as well as between social classes – typically, the poorer the household, the greater the gap). In India, where the disparity between men and women is particularly large, the average time spent by women on unpaid care work is six hours a day; for men it is 36 minutes. But even where the disparity is much smaller, women still do around twice as much unpaid work as men (in North America, for instance, the male mean is just over two hours a day and the female mean is just under four). This unequal division of domestic labour affects women's position in the paid labour market. Where housework is most time-consuming, women cannot engage in paid work at all; where it is slightly less time-consuming they may be limited to part-time, casualised and low-paid jobs. Domestic responsibilities may also make it impossible for women and girls to take up the education and training opportunities which would improve their employment prospects and their earning abilities.

The OECD sees this as a serious problem for developing

countries, since it means that they cannot make full use of women's labour power in their drive to increase economic growth. The report recommends various measures governments can take to address this problem: they can invest in infrastructure to reduce the time housework takes (if more households in Ghana had electricity, fewer women would have to spend time collecting firewood); expand public services like nurseries and daycare centres for the elderly (the report mentions a project in Kenya where mobile crèches were provided for the children of women working on a construction site); introduce 'family-friendly' policies (like flexible hours and parental leave); and try to tackle 'entrenched social norms and gender stereotypes' in an effort to 'de-feminise care-giving' and so encourage men to do more.

It's notable that only the last of these recommendations deals directly with the inequality between the sexes. The others are designed to reduce the burden on women without transferring any of it to men. The difficulty of redistributing unpaid work is suggested by the OECD's own statistics. In rich countries, particularly the welfare states of western Europe, families already have access to time-saving technology, childcare facilities and flexible working hours, but it's still women who do more unpaid care work. Why is this division of labour so persistent? How should we understand it, and what could or should be done about it?

Like all the others discussed in this book, these questions have prompted debate and disagreement among feminists. The rest of this chapter will explore some of the competing analyses, theories and proposals they have put forward. I'll begin, though, by considering how we got to where we are now.

Most human societies have had some kind of sexual division of labour, an arrangement whereby some tasks are assigned to women and others to men. In small-scale traditional societies this arrangement has often been described as egalitarian: the two sexes are economically interdependent, in that each needs the products of the other's labour. There do not seem to be many forms of work which are universally reserved for men or women: the same task – for instance, cultivating corn – may be a man's job in one group and a woman's job in another.

In larger and more complex pre-industrial societies, like those of medieval and early modern Europe, historians have pointed to elements of both hierarchy and reciprocity in the organisation of men's and women's work. Before the Industrial Revolution, most production was based in the household, and much of it was for use rather than for sale. This mode of production required the labour of both sexes: for instance, men might tend the cattle, but women butchered and preserved meat, churned butter and made fat into candles. Women married to artisans or merchants often learnt their husband's trade and assisted with his work; sometimes they acted as their husbands' agents, or took over the business after their husbands died. This arrangement cannot be called gender-egalitarian, because marriage was not a relationship of equals. In England (and later its colonies), married women were subject to 'coverture', a legal provision stipulating that a wife had no existence independent of her husband: her property, earnings and services all belonged to him. Wives who worked alongside their husbands were not equal partners. But the fact that their contribution was needed gave them some leverage: the dependence was mutual rather than all one way.

The Industrial Revolution changed this. Most production gradually moved out of the household and into the factories and mills where men, women and children worked for wages. Consequently, domestic labour became a primarily reproductive rather than productive activity. Instead of making the things her household used (food, beer, clothing, candles), the job of the housewife was to perform the domestic services (such as cooking, cleaning and laundry) that enabled members of the household to keep going out to work. The wages they earned could then be used to buy what would once have been produced 'in-house'. Providing domestic services did not so much become a female responsibility as remain one (the tasks involved were those that women had done in the past); what changed was the conditions in which those services were carried out. In the new industrial economy 'work' and 'home' became distinct domains. A woman who worked for wages was now obliged to carry out domestic tasks like cooking and cleaning when she was not 'at work'; in effect she was required to work a 'second shift'.

Many women did enter the industrial workforce, but their wages were always lower than men's, and this led to conflict. Men argued that they should not have to compete with women who were cheaper to employ, nor settle for lower wages themselves. The idea began to gain ground that men should be paid enough to support a family, while women should prioritise their domestic responsibilities, ideally working outside the home only to supplement the wages of the family breadwinner. This 'male breadwinner with dependent housewife' arrangement is what people today most often mean when they talk about the 'traditional' family or women's 'traditional' role – but historically speaking it is not really 'traditional' at all. Nor was it ever a universal norm in practice. However, it has been argued that it came to be seen as the ideal, not only because it suited men, but also because it served the interests of capitalism. Women whose main occupation was understood to be in the home formed a cheap and convenient 'reserve army of labour' – a Marxist term for a group of un- or under-employed people who can be pulled into the workforce when they are needed (when the economy is booming, for instance, or in wartime, to replace men who are serving in the armed forces) and then pushed out again when recession, or peace, makes them superfluous. In the case of women, this could be justified by saying that they already have a job at home, and that their paid jobs were needed by men with families to support.

But there's a reason why I've been using the past tense. The current neo-liberal and globalised form of capitalism offers other options for reducing costs and maximising profits: for instance, recruiting foreign workers who are willing to accept lower wages, or putting workers on 'zero-hours' contracts, which require them to be available for work, but do not guarantee that they will get any. Companies can also move some of their operations to parts of the world where costs are lower, or invest in technology which lessens their dependence on human labour. The workers whose position has been most dramatically affected by these practices are not women, but first-world working-class men: the industrial manufacturing jobs they once did have moved overseas or been automated, while most newly created jobs are less secure, lower-paid ones in the female-dominated service sector. During the recession that followed the 2008 financial crisis, the Toronto *Globe and Mail* reported that male unemployment in Canada outstripped female unemployment by the largest margin ever recorded.

The old model of a working man supporting his wife and children on a 'family wage' has become increasingly remote from most people's reality, but it remains powerful in the cultural imagination. The recent surge of right-wing populism in the US and many parts of Europe has been fuelled not only by racism and xenophobia, but also by nostalgia for the golden age of the male breadwinner. Much of Donald Trump's appeal to US voters (especially less educated white men) rested on his promise to bring back the well-paid, secure jobs which once gave men authority in their homes and status in their communities. The same desire to return to the past is expressed in a letter written to a Utah newspaper in 2017, calling on state legislators to reject a bill mandating equal pay for men and women on the traditional grounds that men 'need to make enough to support their families and allow the Mother to remain in the home to raise and nurture the children'. This argument presupposes not only that it is desirable for women to be dependent on a male breadwinner, but also that all women have that option. In reality, many women don't: whether because they are single (unmarried, divorced, widowed) or because the men they live with are unemployed, they are obliged to be 'primary breadwinners' themselves. This was also true in the so-called 'golden age' – and indeed for hundreds of years before it. There have always been households that depended on women's earnings. Paying women less than men condemns many of those households to poverty. That is one reason (the other being the basic principle of fairness) why feminists have long supported laws like the one the Utah writer opposes.

But the gender pay gap is not just a consequence of employers paying women less than men for doing the same job (as we see from the fact that it persists in places like Britain, where equal pay laws have been in force for over 40 years). In many areas of the labour market there is sex segregation: women and men do different jobs, and jobs done by women are undervalued precisely because they are done by women. Some are seen as extensions of the unpaid work women do at home, and as such are assumed to require less effort and skill than comparable jobs done by men. This was a central issue in an industrial dispute that helped to pave the way for equal pay legislation in Britain, involving the machinists who made car-seat covers at the Ford plant in Dagenham. These women fought for years to be recognised as skilled rather than unskilled workers – a claim repeatedly dismissed by male managers who probably couldn't even have threaded a sewing machine. Similarly, when I worked in a hospital laundry in the mid-1970s, the men, whose job was loading and unloading washing machines, got paid nearly 50 per cent more than women earned for ironing surgical gowns and nurses' uniforms. (If you don't think ironing demands more skill than loading a washing machine, you clearly haven't done much laundry.)

Another thing that contributes to the pay gap is that many women take time out from paid work, or work part-time, while their children are young. Consequently they earn less than their continuously employed, full-time counterparts, take longer to climb whatever career ladder may exist, and end up with smaller pensions. This way of balancing the competing demands of 'work and family' (or put another way, paid and unpaid work) is often talked about as a 'choice' that individual women make. But the language of 'choice' glosses over the ways in which women's choices are constrained by structural factors they have no control over. Even before they have children, many women will be earning less than their male partners, making it rational in economic terms for the mother to become the primary or full-time parent. Then there are the cultural factors glossed by the OECD as 'entrenched social norms and gender stereotypes'. There is a strong social expectation that the primary carer for children will be their mother: many men either do not want to take that role, or are worried about how employers will perceive them if they do. Last but not least, there is the way in which most paid work is organised, which presupposes that full-time workers can delegate unpaid care work to someone else. A simple illustration is the fact that the standard eight-hour working day is longer than the standard school day, or the standard opening hours of a doctor's surgery.

For feminists it is not enough to say that individual women should have choices. We need to ask why things are arranged in a way that obliges women to make certain choices, and whether we could or should make different arrangements. Many feminist discussions of work have revolved around these questions, but different feminists have approached them in different ways.

Socialist and Marxist feminists have been particularly interested in understanding the place of women's work in the larger economic and social structure. Who benefits from the current arrangements? Their answer is that women's work – both paid and unpaid – does not just benefit their families, but also capitalism and the state. Capitalists get a reserve army of cheap labour, and the services of workers who have been fed and otherwise cared for at no cost to their employer. The state saves on public services, because women do so much care-giving either for nothing or in exchange for very minimal welfare benefits.

This Marxist analysis emphasises the economic value of the domestic services women provide, and one proposal that has come out of it is that the state should compensate women by paying them 'wages for housework'. This might in theory solve two of the problems mentioned earlier: the lack of security and autonomy that results from the house-wife's financial dependence on her husband, and the burden of working an unpaid second shift. But there are other problems it would not solve: it leaves the sexual division of labour unchallenged (if women get paid to do housework, men have even less incentive to share it), and it does not address the argument that doing domestic labour in your own home is inherently so isolating and unrewarding that it should not be anyone's full-time occupation.

Other feminists have opposed the demand for wages for housework, arguing that a more enlightened goal would be to free women from household drudgery. Angela Davis suggested that this could be achieved by shifting from the pre-industrial mode that housework was stuck in (every woman doing the same repetitive tasks in and for her own household) to a more industrial one, in which 'teams of trained and well-paid workers, moving from dwelling to dwelling [with] technologically advanced cleaning machinery, could swiftly and efficiently accomplish what the present-day housewife does so arduously and primitively'. For the radical feminist Shulamith Firestone, the solution was not to industrialise but to collectivise housework and childcare, by creating alternatives to the nuclear family (an institution she saw as central to the oppression of both women and children). She acknowledged that previous experiments along these lines, such as the early Soviet communes, had not always been popular with women; but she rejected the argument that the family was the only institution that could meet people's needs for intimacy and care. In her view the problem with the Soviet experiment was that it had not given proper consideration to those needs: in effect it had just 'drafted women into a male world'.

The same criticism could be made of contemporary capitalist societies: they are keen to integrate women into the labour force (i.e. draft them into the male world of productive work, where they will help to generate economic growth), but efforts to draft men into the female world of care-giving are half-hearted at best: in many cases they do not go much beyond pious exhortations like the OECD's call to tackle 'entrenched social norms and gender stereotypes'. The basic problem is hinted at in something else the OECD says – that care-giving needs to be 'de-feminised' in order to encourage men's participation. Whereas women can expect to gain status by doing the kind of work men do, men perceive 'feminised' care work as something that will lower their status.

It will certainly lower their earnings. Katrine Marçal notes that in Sweden, the care assistant who comforts a dying elderly woman receives an hourly wage of 69 kronor (about £8) – significantly less than, say, an estate agent or a security guard would earn. The OECD talks about 'de-feminising' care-giving, but if we want real equality between the sexes, we will also need to 'demasculinise' the values and assumptions of the workplace, so that it no longer seems 'natural' to pay someone who sells or guards property more than someone who cares for the old, the sick and the dying. More generally, we need to stop basing every aspect of the way work is organised on the assumption that the prototypical worker is a male worker. Even so-called family-friendly policies are usually conceived as making concessions to women's 'special needs'. In 2017, for instance, some researchers in Australia recommended that women's working hours should be cut to a maximum of 34 per week (compared with a male maximum of 47) to compensate for the extra time women spent on 'domestic duties'. If this measure were adopted, its negative consequences – employers trying to avoid hiring women, and men refusing to share the 'domestic duties' ('it's your job, you get time off for it') – would be likely to outweigh the benefits. A more radical approach would be to shorten the working week for everyone, on the assumption that the prototypical worker, regardless of sex, has domestic and caring responsibilities.

Women's relationship to work is not shaped only by institutional and societal factors (such as the laws and policies of the state, the workings of capitalism and the demands of employers), but also by more personal ones. Work-related issues (like time and money and housework and childcare) cause conflict between men and women, and these exemplify the feminist principle 'the personal is political'. At bottom, what's at issue is power: who has the obligation to do what for whom, and who has authority over whom.

When I was growing up, it was common for people to ask married women if their husbands 'let' them go out to work or 'minded' them having a job. (Then, as now, questions based on the opposite premise – 'do you mind your husband having a job?' or 'do you let your husband do housework?' – would have been absurd.) These questions presupposed that women were subject to the authority of their husbands, and that men might see a wife's paid employment as a threat to their authority. Today there is less opposition to women having jobs (in many households their income is essential), but research suggests that it's still quite common for men to resent it if their female partners earn more than they do. Some studies have found that men in this position do less domestic work than traditional 'breadwinners', and are also more likely to have extramarital affairs. This can't be explained in purely economic terms: it has more to do with ideas about masculinity and the 'proper' relationship between the sexes.

I began this chapter by referring to one popular view of feminism as a kind of propaganda campaign urging women to discover the joys of work, while simultaneously devaluing their traditional domestic role. The reality is more complicated. While feminists hold a range of views, they all begin from an understanding that women's dilemma is not 'should I work or stay at home?' (for most women, home *is* a place of work): it's how to negotiate the demands of work, both paid and unpaid, in a world which is organised around men's needs rather than theirs.

4

FEMININITY

In her introduction to *The Second Sex*, Simone de Beauvoir remarked on a paradox:

> All agree in recognising the fact that females exist in the human species; today as always they make up about one half of humanity. And yet we are told that femininity is in danger; we are exhorted to be women, remain women, become women. It would appear, then, that every female human being is not necessarily a woman; to be so considered she must share in that mysterious and threatened reality known as femininity.

In the 1940s when Beauvoir was writing, both popular and much expert wisdom was what we would now call 'essentialist': it held that the universal and unchanging nature of 'Woman' was determined by her biological and reproductive functions. Femininity, it followed, was just the natural expression of femaleness. Beauvoir argued that this was, at the very least, an oversimplification. The word *woman* doesn't just denote a biological category, but more importantly a social one; and to be recognised as a member of the social category 'women' it is not sufficient to have been born female. It is also necessary to have acquired the modes of behaviour and self-presentation which are deemed appropriate for women in a particular time and place. Hence Beauvoir's statement, later on in *The Second Sex*, that 'one is not born, but rather becomes, a woman'. This insight was taken up by the English-speaking feminists of the post-1968 second wave, who made a theoretical distinction between *sex*, meaning biological male/femaleness, and *gender*, meaning culturally defined (or, in the formulation that has since become more common, 'socially constructed') masculinity/femininity.

One important piece of evidence that femininity is socially constructed is that what counts as 'feminine' behaviour is not, in fact, universal and unchanging: it can vary significantly across cultures and over time. Another influential thinker of the mid-twentieth century, the American anthropologist Margaret Mead, drew attention to striking differences in the social roles and personality traits that were considered normal and desirable for men and women in different societies. In *Sex and Temperament*, a study of three traditional societies in Papua New Guinea, which was first published in 1935, Mead compared the Chambuli people, a group in which women took charge and men were seen as the less capable, more passive and more emotional sex, with two other groups, the Arapesh and the Mundugumor, where the same qualities were valued in both sexes. These were different qualities in each case: among the Arapesh both sexes were peaceable, whereas among the Mundugumor they were both aggressive. Mead concluded that human nature was extremely plastic, and that the way it developed in individuals owed more to the influence of culture than to the dictates of biology.

To say this is not to deny that some experiences which are common to many women in all times and places *are* shaped by their biology (for instance, almost all women experience menstruation, and the majority also experience pregnancy and childbirth). But among humans, even the most basic and universal experiences (such as eating, or death, to take two examples which are not sex-specific) are always embedded in culture. How women actually experience biological processes like menstruation or pregnancy will be influenced not only by the nature of the processes themselves, but also by the way those processes are understood and dealt with in the society they belong to.

A great deal of what has to be learnt in the process of becoming a woman has no obvious connection to biological femaleness at all. No biological sex difference can explain, for instance, why my brother's school shirts buttoned in the opposite direction from mine, or why our parents scolded me, but not him, for whistling, or for sitting with my legs apart. These behaviours were not 'unfemale' (I, a female person, was perfectly capable of engaging in them); rather, they were 'unfeminine' – or, as my parents more often said, 'unladylike', i.e. at odds with a particular norm of (middle-class) femininity. The very fact that we can describe a woman's behaviour or appearance as 'unfeminine' without being accused of talking self-contradictory nonsense is another piece of evidence that femininity is different from femaleness. As the writer Susan Brownmiller puts it,

> [femininity] always demands more. It must constantly reassure its audience by a willing demonstration of difference, even when one does not exist in nature, or it must seize and embrace a natural variation and compose a rhapsodic symphony upon the notes.

Femininity is not just a cultural construct but a cultural imposition – a set of expectations, prescriptions and prohibitions, which are enforced through a system of rewards and punishments.

These attempts at enforcement are not, of course, guaranteed to work: many women, past and present, have rejected conventional femininity, and few if any of us embody our culture's idealised notions of the feminine completely and consistently. But while we are free to choose how far we will conform to expectations, the consequences are not a matter of individual choice. As a child I could choose to whistle, but I couldn't prevent the people around me from understanding my behaviour as 'unladylike' and judging it accordingly (which is to say, negatively).

What about masculinity? Isn't that also a cultural construct, something male-born people have to learn the rules of (e.g. 'boys don't cry', or 'real men don't show their feelings')? Don't men also get rewarded or punished for conforming to or deviating from the masculine norm? In short, isn't the binary gender system limiting and oppressive for everyone? The short answer to these questions is 'yes': if femininity is socially constructed then the same must be true of masculinity. These are relational terms, defined by contrast with one another. However, it doesn't necessarily follow that they should be thought of as simply the proverbial 'two sides of the same coin'. As Beauvoir observed in *The Second Sex*, their relationship may appear to be perfectly symmetrical, but on closer examination it is not: 'Man represents both the positive and the neutral, as is indicated by the common use of *man* to designate human beings in general; whereas woman represents only the negative, defined by limiting criteria, without reciprocity.'

Gender, from this perspective, is not just a system of social categorisation based on a contrast between two equal-but-opposite terms: it is a hierarchy in which the masculine outranks the feminine. While some gender distinctions (like the placement of shirt buttons) seem arbitrary and trivial, others can be linked more directly to the social system in which men are expected to exercise power while women play a secondary, supporting role. Masculinity is active, assertive, rational, strong and courageous; femininity is passive, submissive, emotional, weak and in need of protection. The qualities women are encouraged to cultivate are also the qualities that are used to justify their inferior social status. It is undoubtedly true that many individual men and boys experience the demands of masculinity as oppressive, and for some they are deeply damaging. Men who are judged insufficiently masculine can face severe sanctions: at the extreme, the penalty may be death. But while feminists acknowledge that the system has negative consequences for both sexes, they do not want to lose sight of the larger purpose it serves – it is part of the apparatus that maintains men's collective position of dominance over women.

Feminists also, of course, want to change the system – though, as usual, they have a range of views on what to do about it. Some feminists are gender 'abolitionists', advocating a world in which, to quote Shulamith Firestone, 'genital differences between human beings would no longer matter culturally', while others would like individuals to be free to choose from a more diverse array of gender identities. There are also many feminists who are less interested in overthrowing the binary gender system, and more concerned to challenge the narrowness and rigidity of its current norms.

In the rest of this chapter I will look more closely at two sets of questions about femininity that have featured prominently in both feminist theoretical analysis and feminist political activism since the 1960s. One set of questions concerns something which almost all feminists have seen as oppressive: the impact on girls and women of normative expectations about their bodily appearance. The other, which I will begin with, concerns the way the norms of femininity (and masculinity) are acquired during the formative years of childhood.

Since Simone de Beauvoir expounded it in 1949, the anti-essentialist argument that 'one is not born a woman' has faced repeated challenges, and one of the great battlegrounds in this debate is the question of child development. Those who argue that male–female differences are products of nature rather than nurture very often appeal to evidence showing that these differences emerge very early in life, before children become aware of social norms and expectations. They also point to the apparent failure of non-sexist child-rearing practices to eliminate the differences. However they are socialised, it seems, girls and boys just 'naturally' prefer to do, wear and play with different things.

This 'only natural' argument was challenged during the feminist second wave, and was briefly out of fashion; but in recent decades it has become popular again, influentially championed by the evolutionary psychologists whose account of human nature I mentioned in chapter 2. Evolutionary psychologists explain differences between the sexes with reference to the purposes they would hypothetically have served among our earliest human ancestors, and it sometimes seems as if there is nothing that cannot be fitted into this narrative. In 2007, a group of researchers even suggested that the attraction of the colour pink for little girls in the twenty-first century might be a product of nature rather than culture, reflecting the importance of pink (the colour of many edible berries) for the female gatherers of human prehistory. Conversely, boys' preference for blue might go back to the time when prehistoric hunters spent hours scanning the sky. But historians pointed out a flaw in this story: there is nothing ancient about the association of pink with girls and blue with boys. On the contrary, as recently as the early twentieth century pink was considered a masculine colour (a milder version of red, and as such particularly suitable for little boys), while blue was regarded as more feminine (in European religious painting, for instance, it is traditionally the colour of the Virgin Mary's robes).

Why are we so receptive to the kinds of stories evolutionary psychology tells? In part, perhaps, because gender distinctions often do present themselves to us in everyday life as fixed and intractable. If you are a parent whose daughter insists, despite all your objections, that everything she owns must be pink, it is easy to feel that her intransigence must be produced by something more profound than a mere cultural norm. We tend to think of nature or biology as 'deep', and culture as shallow and superficial. But this is a mistake: culture is also 'deep'. The process of creating social beings is, as the pioneering sociologist Emile Durkheim remarked, a highly coercive one, involving 'a continual effort to impose upon the child ways of seeing, thinking and acting which he himself [sic] would not have arrived at spontaneously'. Many feminists over the years have sought to document the processes which impose gendered ways of seeing, thinking and acting on children from the moment of their birth.

Some of this documentation comes from controlled scientific studies measuring, for instance, how long mothers spend verbally interacting with young children (typically this research has found that they interact more with girls than with boys), or how a child's sex affects adults' assessments of their physical abilities (we tend to overestimate what boys can manage while underestimating what girls of the same age can do). This body of research provides evidence that male and female children really are treated differently from the very beginning, in ways which do have the potential to affect their subsequent development. It also offers evidence of the phenomenon the psychologist Cordelia Fine calls 'parenting with half-changed minds'. Even adults who consciously oppose gender stereotyping, and who genuinely believe they are treating their sons and their daughters identically, still seem to be influenced at a subconscious level by stereotypes like 'girls are more verbally expressive and boys are more physically adventurous'.

Another psychologist, Bronwyn Davies, studied preschool children's own attempts to make sense of the differences between girls and boys. She observed that they were receiving mixed messages from adults: liberal parents and teachers discouraged 'extreme' expressions of masculinity and femininity – they didn't want ultra-aggressive, emotionally insensitive boys, or girls who were passive shrinking violets in frilly dresses – but at the same time they demanded that their children should be intelligible as gendered beings, and were uncomfortable if a girl's behaviour was too boyish, or if a boy's taste in clothes or toys was too girly. (In a similar vein, Cordelia Fine quotes some parents explaining the compromise they made when their son begged them for a Barbie doll: they bought him NASCAR Barbie, one of the less feminised versions of the popular toy.)

It is not hard to sympathise with parents like these, caught as they are between their desire for the world to be different and their obligation to ensure that their children can thrive in the world as it currently exists. The resulting mixed messages become part of the puzzle that children themselves have to solve. Bronwyn Davies emphasises that even pre-schoolers are actively engaged in the process of gender socialisation – they are not just passive recipients of adult instruction. And the adults who care for them are not the only source of the knowledge they bring to bear on the task. By the time Davies met them, her young subjects had already developed a range of roles both inside and outside the family: they were pupils at pre-school, members of child peer groups, consumers of mass media and of products like food, clothes and toys. In all these capacities, they were absorbing information about what it meant to be a girl or a boy.

This learning process has been documented in observational diaries kept by feminist parents. In the early 1980s, the

German lawyer and feminist Marianne Grabrucker published a detailed record of the first three years of her daughter Anneli's life, paying attention to all the ways in which relatives, friends and strangers instructed the little girl in the rules of gender-appropriate behaviour and rewarded her for performing femininity – complimenting her on looking pretty, or praising her for being helpful and deferring to the boys she played with. Inspired by this example, in 2011 the British journalists Ros Ball and James Millar set up a Twitter account, @GenderDiary, in which they reflected on their experiences as parents of a girl and a boy. They noticed systematic differences in the way their two children were treated and talked about as they went through the same developmental stages. For instance, when they took their baby son (the younger of the two) to the clinic, staff often commented positively on how big he was. He wasn't any bigger than his sister had been at his age, but his size was remarked on more often than hers had been. Ball and Millar also realised that when the word 'big' was applied to their daughter it was more likely to refer to her behaving in a 'grown-up' way than to her literal physical size. Largeness is seen as a neutral or positive quality in boys, but a negative one in girls. This norm is even reflected in the construction of clothing for young children. Not only are girls' and boys' clothes generally distinguished by their surface style (colours, motifs, degree of fussy detail), many brands also produce girls' clothes which are smaller than the clothes they sell for boys, beginning at an age when there are still no significant sex differences in average height or weight.

When people cite the 'failure' of non-sexist parenting as

evidence that nature trumps nurture, feminists reply that they are underestimating not only the effects of parents' subconsciously held beliefs, but also the strength of all the other cultural influences that affect children's development, and which could only be prevented from doing so if parents denied their children a normal life (no school, no friends, no TV or internet, no mass-produced clothes and toys). Some parents have undertaken very radical experiments: in 2011, for example, a Canadian couple announced their intention to raise their youngest child Storm (whose sex they declined to reveal), 'gender-neutrally'. In pursuit of this goal they have chosen to move outside the cultural mainstream, living 'off-grid' and home-schooling their three children. For most parents, however, this is not a practical option, and it also has political limitations, in that it is an individual solution to a social problem. To address the larger issues, it is necessary to campaign for change within the mainstream.

Numerous campaigns of this kind were set up by parents in the 1970s, and they have recently made something of a comeback. In 2012, a discussion on the British online forum Mumsnet prompted activists to organise a campaign called 'Let Toys Be Toys', which aims to persuade retailers to stop labelling toys by gender in their stores and catalogues. There is now a similar campaign to de-gender the marketing of children's books. Criticism of the stereotyping which pervades children's films and TV has led to the creation of more assertive female protagonists in animated features like Disney's *Brave* and *Frozen* – though research shows that male characters still get more speaking time overall, and the new generation of princesses still represent a conventional ideal of feminine beauty (typically white, youthful, slender, with long hair and big eyes). Although they are animations rather than actual people, critics point out that the characteristics of their two-dimensional bodies are only exaggerated versions of what real girls and women are told they should aspire to.

This is one aspect of the social construction of femininity that has prompted criticism throughout feminism's history. In chapter 2, I quoted Mary Wollstonecraft's complaint, made in the 1790s, that women were encouraged to concentrate on perfecting their bodies rather than their minds because they were 'taught from infancy that beauty is woman's sceptre'. The first-wave feminists who fought for access to education and the right to vote were also critical of nineteenth-century feminine dress codes: they particularly deplored the fashion for corsets with tight lacing that were designed to produce an unnaturally tiny waist, worn with heavy petticoats and cumbersome skirts. In the US in 1849, Amelia Bloomer introduced an alternative of her own invention – the 'Bloomer outfit', a sort of pantaloons-and-tunic combination; in Britain in the 1880s the Rational Dress Society also championed split pants, in part to allow women to participate more easily in the increasingly popular activity of bicycling. Though inevitably accused of wanting to destroy natural sex differences, these reformers were actually criticising the artificial and restrictive nature of Victorian femininity: there was nothing 'natural' about corsets and crinolines.

The Women's Liberation Movement that emerged during

the 1960s also wanted to liberate women from oppressive and unrealistic standards of beauty, and from the idea that a woman's worth was determined by her ability to produce herself as a desirable object for men's consumption. Some of the movement's earliest and most visible actions were protests against beauty pageants, where women contestants were, as the protestors saw it, paraded like cattle at a market. Like their nineteenth-century predecessors, these feminists criticised dress norms that restricted women's freedom of movement, or which caused chronic physical discomfort (for instance, the wearing of girdles and high-heeled shoes); but they were equally if not more concerned with the psychological damage inflicted on women by the pressure to perfect their appearance. This concern became even stronger in the 1990s, when commentators pointed to the rising incidence of eating disorders and the growth in demand for cosmetic surgery as signs that all was not well with the generation of women who had grown up with equal rights. 'The more legal and material hindrances women have broken through,' wrote Naomi Wolf in her book *The Beauty Myth*, 'the more strictly and heavily and cruelly images of female beauty have come to weigh upon us.'

The philosopher Heather Widdows believes that the pressure on women to conform to exacting beauty standards – or, as she calls them, 'beauty demands' – has become even more extreme since 1990. The same standards are increasingly applied to women globally, and the pressure to meet them lasts longer, beginning well before puberty (a survey by Girlguiding UK found that seven out of ten girls aged between seven and eleven reported feeling anxiety and shame about their appearance), and continuing long after menopause. Achieving the desired look requires both effort and technological assistance: the ideal woman is supposed to be young (or young-looking in relation to her actual age), thin or slim (a particularly favoured body shape combines full breasts and buttocks with a small waist), golden-skinned (a norm which requires most Black women to lighten their skin while white women must tan theirs), with a body that is firm, smooth and almost entirely hairless. Desirable facial features include prominent cheekbones and large eyes (the last of these norms has made eye-lift surgery increasingly common in parts of Asia). Widdows notes that meeting these expectations is presented as a moral imperative: you 'owe it to yourself' not to 'let yourself go'; you should make the effort 'because you're worth it'. Failure to measure up to the ideal is thus experienced by many women as a moral failure, a judgement not only on their physical worth but on their character.

Some feminists might argue that Widdows's own language is moralistic and judgemental, and that she denies women's status as autonomous agents who can decide for themselves what is in their best interests. If we oppose attempts to tell women what they can or can't do with their reproductive organs, why is it acceptable to tell them what they should or shouldn't do with other parts of their bodies? With beauty as with motherhood, feminists should support women's right to choose. In the immortal words of the singer Cher, 'if I want to put my tits on my back, it's nobody's business but my own.'

Once again, though, the counter-argument is that our

choices are not made in a vacuum, but in response to social pressures which individuals can neither control nor disregard. There are clear rewards for complying with the norms that define an acceptably feminine appearance, and clear penalties for non-compliance. For instance, studies show that employers are more likely to hire, promote and offer higher salaries to 'attractive' women (and men too, but the effect is larger for women). This system of value is something most of us will have internalised long before we are able to make consequential life decisions. Appearance-based discrimination has been observed among children as young as three: they judge peers with certain physical characteristics (e.g. being fat) as being less desirable as friends and playmates. If the choices we make as adults are informed by beliefs and desires formed so early in life, can they really be regarded as 'free'?

Another objection to the 'choice' argument is that it echoes the beauty industry's own protestations that it is only giving the customer what she wants, when in fact, like other branches of consumer capitalism, it has a long history of creating new needs, desires and insecurities that it can then exploit to generate more profits. (Did anyone worry about 'feminine freshness', or 'free radicals', before advertising brought these things to their attention?) In the global South, the desires and insecurities being exploited are also bound up with the history of colonialism and racism. Corporations based in Europe and North America have flooded the markets of Africa, Asia and Latin America with skin-lightening preparations that do not meet the safety standards of the rich world; some are sufficiently toxic to put regular users at increased risk of developing cancers, neurological problems and kidney disease. Even when they are not literally toxic, the promotion of these products reinforces the toxic effects of racism, which is responsible for creating the hierarchy of value in which fair skin is preferred to dark skin.

It is not only the beauty industry that influences our ideas about what female bodies should look like; concern has also been expressed about the growing influence of pornography. In 2017 there were reports that an increasing number of girls in Britain were being referred to specialists in labiaplasty because of their unhappiness with the appearance of their genitals. In 2015–16 the NHS carried out 150 labiaplasty operations on girls under the age of fifteen. It is possible to argue that this benefited the individuals concerned by relieving real and damaging anxieties; but it is hard for a feminist to be uncritical of the culture that produces those anxieties in adolescent and pre-adolescent girls.

The negative effects of femininity on women have received critical attention during every wave of feminism, but it is also true that this stance has provoked disagreement among feminists. There has always been a strand in feminist thinking which maintains that there is more to femininity than subordination. Traditionally female activities and rituals can be a source of pleasure, providing outlets for women's creativity, and opportunities for female bonding; feminine qualities like empathy and nurturance are valuable and should be celebrated.

One recently influential defence of femininity has been offered by the trans feminist Julia Serano, who criticises feminism for reproducing the institutionalised preference of patriarchal cultures for masculinity. She points out that while feminism has made 'masculine' qualities and activities more acceptable for women and girls, the reverse has not happened: our culture remains deeply uncomfortable with any display of femininity in men or boys. The discussion of non-sexist parenting earlier in this chapter offers support for this observation. Parents may be happy for their daughters to climb trees and build model spaceships, but many are more ambivalent about their sons' requests for Barbie dolls. However, other feminists might give a different account of what's ultimately behind this difference. Parents who discourage certain interests and behaviours in boys may be motivated not by prejudice against femininity, but by awareness that an insufficiently masculine boy or man is potentially a target for other men's violence. This male-on-male gender-policing serves to defend the hierarchical system that requires men to behave not just differently from women, but in a way that enacts and symbolises dominance over women. Women who refuse to perform femininity are rebels, but men who flout the norms of masculinity are traitors, and the severity of the punishment reflects that.

As I noted in chapter one, male dominance is a pervasive and complex phenomenon with very deep historical roots, and it is hardly surprising if feminism has not yet eliminated it. That doesn't mean that it's a law of nature and that resistance to it is futile, nor does it mean that nothing has been achieved. In some communities, in some respects, the norms of femininity and masculinity have become considerably less rigid over the last 50 years. But it could also be argued that some norms have become *more* rigid, and more negative in their effects. In the next chapter, I consider feminist approaches to another area of experience where change has been real, but also partial, and not always unequivocally positive: sex.

5

SEX

The publishing sensation of 2012 was E. L. James's *Fifty Shades of Grey*, an erotic novel by a previously unknown author, which chronicled the relationship between Christian Grey, a billionaire 'dom' (the dominant partner in sexual encounters governed by the rules of BDSM), and Anastasia Steele, a young college graduate who is still a virgin when the two first meet. The book was the first volume in a trilogy, by the end of which the couple are married with a child. Despite the trappings of 'kink' (chains, whips, spanking), it is in essence a conventional heterosexual romance. However, it was the kink aspect that made *Fifty Shades* a cultural phenomenon, prompting pundits of all kinds to ask what its extraordinary appeal to women readers said about the position of women in the twenty-first century. Did it say, for instance, that feminism has not changed the fundamental and eternal truth that girls just wanna be dominated by older, richer, more powerful men? Or do today's women get pleasure from fantasies of female powerlessness precisely because they are now, in reality, so powerful? Was the popularity of these books (which spawned a whole genre, dubbed 'mommy porn' by the media) a sign that women have been liberated to explore their own desires without shame, or was it worrying evidence of their continued susceptibility to representations which make violence against women 'sexy'?

This question divided feminist commentators (though they were more or less united in hating the books). Whereas some argued that relationships based on male dominance and female submission are inherently problematic, others, while agreeing that *Fifty Shades* was problematic, maintained that the problem was its misrepresentation of BDSM (which is based on a contract between equal partners, whereas Ana in the book is not Christian's equal). One writer who took this view declared herself 'fully in support of anyone doing whatever (safe, consensual) thing they want to do to get themselves off. Feminists for Orgasms!' But others criticised this kind of 'orgasm politics' for taking no account of the way sexual desires are shaped by the social and political context. 'Women cope with male violence and oppression', wrote one, 'by eroticizing male dominance.'

The debate about *Fifty Shades* is one recent instance of a larger debate about sex which has gone on, in some form or other, throughout the history of feminism. As Carole Vance wrote in 1984, sex for women is 'simultaneously a domain of restriction, repression and danger, as well as a domain of exploration, pleasure and agency'. If feminists focus only on the 'pleasure' side they risk ignoring the reality of male violence and oppression, but if they focus only on the 'danger' side they risk ignoring women's experience of sex as something actively desired and enjoyed. Few feminists would disagree with Vance's point that these two dimensions exist, and that feminism must address them both. But feminists have not agreed on what the balance between the two should be, and on some issues there are deep divisions between those who describe their position as 'sex-positive' (like the 'Feminists for Orgasms!' writer) and those who put more emphasis on the way in which sex becomes, in patriarchal societies, a site of oppression and violence.

Historians of the first wave generally agree that feminist discussions of sex in the nineteenth and early twentieth centuries were dominated by the impulse to protect women from sexual danger and to reform 'the beast in man' (though there were some feminists who contested this, campaigning for women's access to birth control, abortion, sex education and the freedom to have sex outside marriage). The second wave, however, took sexual politics in a new direction. Emerging in the late 1960s, the early Women's Liberation Movement drew energy and inspiration from a counterculture that had rebelled against the sexual conservatism of mainstream society, rejecting its attempts to confine sex within the narrow limits of bourgeois marriage and reproduction. This 'sexual revolution' was part of a utopian political project: not only was having more, freer sex considered positive in itself, it was also thought of as a means to other positive political ends (as is suggested by slogans like 'make love, not war'). For women, sexual freedom had particularly radical implications, because sex had so often been the ground on which women's freedom was restricted. The risks and punishments associated with sexual activity outside marriage were greater for women than for men: not only a woman's sexual behaviour, but all her public behaviour (what she did, where she went, who she met) had to be policed in order to avoid damaging her all-important 'reputation'. Lynne Segal, herself a member of the generation that rebelled against these restrictions, says that for the women of the early second wave, 'women's rights to sexual pleasure and fulfilment, on their own terms, symbolised their rights to autonomy and selfhood.' It was not, in other words, just about the sex.

But the sex was certainly part of what it was about. At the same time as their behaviour was being policed to prevent them having illicit sex, women were also being informed by medical and other experts that they were by nature less interested in sex than men, as well as naturally passive and inclined to monogamy (whereas men were naturally promiscuous). Feminists were quick to point out the contradictions in this view of female sexuality, and keen to demonstrate its inaccuracy. One recurring theme in early second-wave writing was the exploration, and celebration, of all the desires women were not supposed to have – whether for the kind of anonymous, commitment-free heterosexual encounter which the heroine of Erica Jong's 1973 novel *Fear of Flying* called 'the zipless fuck', or for sexual relationships with other women. Another recurring theme, though, was the failure of the sexual revolution to deliver pleasure and fulfilment on women's terms. In 1971, Alix Kates Shulman remarked that women in the radical counterculture felt as much pressure as suburban housewives to fake the orgasms which they were not actually experiencing. She added: 'The explanation that it is all simply a result of ignorance, men's and women's, will not do.'

Another feminist, Anne Koedt, had made the same point a year earlier in a widely read short paper entitled 'The myth of the vaginal orgasm'. She pointed out that scientific research (such as the work of the sexologists Masters and

Johnson, published in the mid-1960s) had confirmed that the female orgasm originates in the clitoris, not the vagina. Yet psychoanalysts, therapists and purveyors of popular advice continued to maintain that a 'mature' woman who had fully accepted her own femininity could and should experience orgasm through penis-in-vagina intercourse. Koedt suggested that what kept this idea in circulation, despite its being contradicted by both science and experience, was the fact that it served men's interests. Women had been 'defined sexually in terms of what pleases men', and if they didn't find intercourse satisfying they were told that there was something wrong with them. The way forward, Koedt declared, was to 'create new guidelines which take into account mutual sexual enjoyment … We must demand that if certain sexual positions now defined as "standard" are not mutually conducive to orgasm, they no longer be defined as standard.'

Almost 50 years later, the problem that Koedt and her contemporaries identified – that sex was defined in terms of what men, rather than women, got pleasure from – has still not been solved. In the early 1990s, a team of British researchers who conducted in-depth interviews with a representative sample of young men and women found that 'sex' was still understood by almost everyone as meaning penis-in-vagina intercourse. Clitoral stimulation might or might not be used as 'foreplay', but the sex act proper began with penetration and ended with ejaculation. Whereas the male orgasm was taken for granted, the female orgasm was not. Similar attitudes and practices are documented in a much more recent (2016) book from the US, Peggy

Orenstein's *Girls and Sex*. Orenstein, too, found that boys' pleasure was treated as 'a given', whereas that of girls was 'secondary, an afterthought'. (This rule extended beyond intercourse: the girls she interviewed told her that they routinely performed oral sex, and that boys expected this; but the favour was very rarely returned, and most girls did not question this asymmetry.)

Orenstein believes that this issue could be addressed through better sex education: the information young people currently receive (at least in the US) tends to be focused on bodily mechanics (in the case of the female body the emphasis is often more on reproduction than on sex), and this leaves no space to talk about desires, feelings and relationships. Both at school and at home, girls are more likely to be warned about the dangers of sex (pregnancy, STIs and rape) than engaged in a discussion of its pleasures. For the many young Americans whose school sex education programme is 'abstinence-based', the only advice they get is 'don't'. And like many contemporary commentators, Orenstein worries about the source to which many young people are turning in an attempt to fill the gap: pornography.

Whether pornography represents 'pleasure' or 'danger' is one of the questions that divides feminists most starkly. There are long-standing arguments between those who see its representation of sex as an incitement to real-world sexual violence and abuse ('porn is the theory, rape is the practice') and those who see it as a valuable resource, enabling people – especially women and members of sexual minorities – to explore their desires, learn about their bodies, and see themselves represented as sexual beings. Feminists who take the latter view may acknowledge that women are not well served by most commercial pornography, which is designed for heterosexual men. But the answer, they argue, is not to oppose pornography as such, but rather to exploit its potential by demanding, or producing, less male-centred and sexist alternatives. They also worry that opposition to porn puts feminists on the same side as religious conservatives who would like to censor all representations of sex, not to mention all real-world expressions of sexuality which do not meet their narrow moral standards. In response, anti-porn feminists say that their overriding concern is not with sexual morality as conservatives understand it, but with the abuse of women, children and men both inside the pornography industry and in the wider society that consumes its products.

These arguments featured prominently in the feminist 'sex wars' of the 1980s, and they have re-emerged in response to more recent developments. The internet has made all kinds of pornography more easily accessible (research suggests that while men still consume more porn than women, both sexes are seeing more of it than they did in the 1980s, and encountering it at younger ages), and many other elements of what used to be a hidden and stigmatised subculture have now been brought into the cultural mainstream. Strip clubs, rebranded as 'Gentlemen's clubs', have left their old seedy premises and established a presence on Britain's high streets, while pole dancing is sold to women as a sexy way of keeping fit. Pre-adolescent girls wear T-shirts bearing the legend 'pornstar', and actual porn stars have become popular culture icons.

This is what some feminists have named 'porn culture', meaning not simply a culture where porn exists, but one where it is normalised and culturally pervasive. And some feminists argue that the rise of porn culture is linked to the rise of 'rape culture' – again, not just a culture where rape exists, but a culture that normalises and enables it. It might sound strange to talk about the culture 'enabling' rape when the law defines it as a violent crime second only to murder. But most rape prosecutions do not end in a conviction, and many incidents are not prosecuted, or even reported, because cultural myths and stereotypes (like 'once they're aroused men can't help themselves' and 'women say no when they don't mean it') stop many people from seeing rape as 'real' unless it happens at knifepoint in a dark alley. The same myths also prompt people to look for reasons to blame the victim rather than the perpetrator. While many factors contribute to this situation, some feminist campaigners believe that porn culture is one. You don't have to believe that porn directly causes rape to see it as one repository of the myths that enable so many men to rape with impunity.

As in the 1980s, though, other feminists reject this argument, insisting that it is possible, and indeed necessary, to oppose rape and rape culture while also asserting women's right to be actively and visibly sexual. This is the attitude expressed in the recent phenomenon of 'slutwalks', anti-rape protests at which some women wear stereotypically sexy clothes to contest the idea that women who dress or behave in certain ways are inviting or provoking sexual violence (the first slutwalk was organised in 2011 after a police officer in Toronto told a group of students that they should 'avoid dressing like sluts' for their own safety).

Arguments about the effects of porn culture do not all focus on the question of whether it contributes to the prevalence of rape. Peggy Orenstein, for instance, is more concerned about the way it shapes ideas about what is pleasurable in consensual relationships. This concern is not confined to older feminists who did not grow up with the culture they criticise. In 2015 a woman posted anonymously on Twitter: 'I'm 23. Mine is the first generation to be exposed to online porn from a young age. We learnt what sex is from watching strangers on the internet.' She went on to list various porn-inspired things that her male sexual partners had done without asking her (such as pulling her hair and ejaculating on her face); pressured her into doing despite her reluctance (such as having anal sex); or criticised her for refusing to do (such as participating in group sex). None of these were things she herself desired, yet she recalls that 'on every single occasion I felt guilty for not being a "cool girl". I was letting him down. I was a prude.'

This writer is suggesting that porn culture has brought with it new expectations of female heterosexual performance, which women like herself have internalised, and feel inadequate if they do not meet. The 'cool girl'/'prude' distinction may look completely different from the more traditional one between 'nice girls' and 'sluts', but it functions in a similar way: in both cases, the fear of being on the wrong side of the line spurs women to police their own behaviour. Rather than liberating women to pursue sexual pleasure on their own terms, this just replaces one oppressive standard ('nice girls don't') with another ('cool girls do whatever men want'). But as ever, there are other feminists who say that they do find pleasure and fulfilment in the sexual practices which the Twitter writer rejects, and that pornography has enhanced their experience by opening up new erotic possibilities.

Clearly, women's sexual desires vary. But in dealing with that reality, as Lisa Downing, a feminist scholar who describes her approach as 'neither sex-positive nor sex-negative, but *sex-critical*', has argued, feminist discussions often become polarised between two positions. One, channelling the utopian spirit of the sexual revolution, holds that sex is good in and of itself, and any kind of sex that any woman finds pleasurable must automatically be liberating and politically progressive ('Feminists for Orgasms!'). The other maintains that (hetero)sex under patriarchy is inherently oppressive, and any pleasure women derive from it must be considered suspect. Downing's own view is that both these arguments are too simple, and that 'all forms of sexuality and all sexual representations should be equally susceptible to critical thinking and interrogation.'

What feminist opponents of porn culture criticise is not just pornography, but the mainstreaming of the sex industry more generally. This raises questions not only about women's position as consumers of the industry's products, but also about their involvement in it as 'sex workers', an umbrella term which covers a range of occupations from glamour modelling and stripping to prostitution, the direct sale of sexual services. This is another issue on which feminists are deeply divided. Is selling sex just a job like any other, problematic only insofar as it is criminalised and socially stigmatised, or is it a form of sexual exploitation which will always be incompatible with the principles of sexual equality and justice?

Feminist interventions on the issue of prostitution have a long history. In Britain in the late 1860s, feminists set up a national campaign for the repeal of the Contagious Diseases Acts, laws which allowed the police in certain military garrison towns to arrest any woman suspected of being a 'common prostitute' and force her to submit to a medical inspection (if she refused she could be imprisoned, and if she was found to have an infection she could be involuntarily confined to a hospital). The manifesto issued by the campaigners denounced the law for discriminating against its targets on the basis of their sex and class, denying them basic rights and subjecting them to a degrading procedure which might well be called 'instrumental rape'. Feminists also attacked the law for giving official sanction to the sexual double standard. Without men's demand for it there would be no prostitution, but the stigma of prostitution and the legal penalties associated with it fell only on the women involved.

Victorian feminists were often censorious about prostitution, but they understood that women's voluntary involvement in it was most often motivated by economic need: in a society which severely restricted women's access to other forms of work it was often 'the best-paid industry'. (They also knew that the involvement of some women and girls was not voluntary: coercion and trafficking existed then as now.) But some middle-class feminists also saw the existence of this trade as an overt expression of the misogyny whose more genteel forms permeated their own relationships with men. The campaign leader Josephine Butler, addressing men of her own class, said: 'You cannot hold us in honour so long as you drag our sisters in the mire. As you are unjust and cruel to them, you will become unjust and cruel to us.'

Feminists who oppose prostitution today have made a similar analysis of its workings as an economic and social institution. They argue that the existence of a market where men can buy sexual consent (that is, pay for sexual acts which the other party would not choose to perform without payment) both reflects and reinforces the inequality between the sexes, and undermines the principle that sex should be an exchange based on mutual desire. Many feminists who make these arguments are supporters of the 'Nordic model' (so called because it was pioneered in Sweden, and has also been adopted in Norway and Iceland), in which the law prohibits the purchase of sexual services, while decriminalising the act of selling them. This is intended both to transfer the legal sanctions associated with commercial sex from prostitutes (mainly women) to sex-buyers (overwhelmingly men), and to reduce the overall demand: as a Swedish law enforcement officer told the writer Kat Banyard, buying sex, like speeding, is something many men do 'because they can', and they will stop if they know it has legal and social costs. The model also includes provisions to support those involved in prostitution and enable them, if they wish, to move out of it. Studies suggest that many do want to exit, but they often face obstacles, from substance abuse problems to the difficulty of getting other work when you have criminal convictions for soliciting.

Other feminists, however, argue that the Nordic model is based on moralistic and patronising attitudes to women who sell sex, and that a more progressive approach would recognise that 'sex work is work'. Selling sex is in principle no different from selling, say, beauty treatments (which may also require intimate contact between worker and client) or serving coffee (customers can be obnoxious to baristas, too), or cleaning toilets (which also involves dealing with strangers' bodily effluvia). Feminists who take this view often make the same observation I made in chapter 3: that doing things you don't enjoy in exchange for the money you need to pay your bills is the lot of most of the world's working women. If a woman sees prostitution as a rational economic choice, what right has anyone else to criticise her, let alone campaign for measures that will put her out of a job? From this perspective, feminists should support sex workers by campaigning for improvements in their working conditions – and, in particular, for the decriminalisation or legalisation of prostitution (the difference is that 'legalised' prostitution is regulated by the state). Feminists on this side of the argument point out that women engaged in an illegal activity cannot easily take action to reduce the risks involved: they will hesitate to report abusive men to the police, or to complain about working practices that compromise their health and safety. If the selling of sex were put on the same footing as the selling of any other service, it would make women safer, reduce the stigma attached to their occupation, and open up opportunities for them to take control of their working lives. They could set up small businesses or co-operatives with other women, instead of depending on the pimps and organised criminals who are powerful players in the illegal trade.

Their opponents respond that the risks involved in selling sex cannot be reduced to an acceptable level, because so many of them arise from the nature of the job rather than its legal status. The most serious occupational hazard of pros-titution is being assaulted or even killed by a buyer during the private sexual encounter that is central to the business, whether or not it is illegal. Campaigners also argue that in countries which have legalised prostitution, like Germany and the Netherlands, the promised benefits for women have not materialised. Rather, the industry has been freed to reorganise along neoliberal capitalist lines, with wealthy investors and entrepreneurs, not workers, reaping the financial rewards. Women selling sex in Germany's legal-ised 'megabrothels' have not become employees with rights and benefits (let alone co-owners and managers): they are instead treated as self-employed contractors, paying the management a fee for each shift they work, which means that they must service several men before they start earning money for themselves.

It is not only in the commercial sex trade that women exchange sex for money or other benefits. Both first- and early second-wave feminists sometimes argued that mar-riage was only a legal and respectable form of prostitution, in which wives provided sexual and domestic services to their husbands in exchange for their financial support (under the law as it then stood, wives could not withhold consent to sex: rape in marriage did not become a crime in England until 1991). Several former prostitutes told Kat Banyard that the idea of sex as a tradable commodity was one they had understood long before they began to sell sex for money. One woman explained that from an early age she had seen her sexuality not as a part of herself, but as 'a thing men wanted from me and which I had to give them to feel that I was worth something'. Another said her experience had taught her that as a woman 'your primary power is your sexual power'. Is this understanding of women's sexuality only a problem when the terms of the trade are exploitative, or is the heterosexual contract in which sex becomes a commodity – something women offer to men in exchange for upkeep, money, power or self-esteem – inherently problematic?

While some feminists have put their energies into reclaiming heterosexuality by creating new, more equal ways for men and women to relate to one another sexually and socially, others have advocated alternatives to it. One alternative is refusing sex entirely. There was once a group of US radical feminists who called themselves 'Women Against Sex', and whose manifesto proclaimed that 'there is no way out of the practice of sexuality except *out*'. People who today identify as asexual are not usually motivated by the same analysis, but they do arguably represent a challenge to the prevailing assumption that sexuality and sexual activity are essential for human flourishing. Other feminists have suggested that sexual (and other intimate) relationships with women represent a positive alternative to the heterosexual contract. The French feminist Monique Wittig argued in

1981 that a lesbian is not a woman: she maintained that what defines women as a social category is their subordination to men within the heterosexual economy, and that lesbians, however precarious their position, are outside that system.

A year earlier, in an article entitled 'Compulsory heterosexuality and lesbian existence', the poet Adrienne Rich had argued that heterosexuality should be seen not simply as a choice or a natural inclination, but as a political institution whose dictates most women had little choice but to comply with. Though the taboo on homosexuality applied to both sexes, the pressure to engage in heterosexual relationships (ruling out not only lesbianism but also celibacy) bore especially heavily on women because of their economic dependence on marriage. Rich asked her readers to consider the possibility that this pressure, and the persecution of women who resisted it, reflected a well-founded fear that if they were truly free to choose, many women would choose each other.

Rich's article was written, in part, to challenge the marginalisation of lesbians and lesbianism in the theory and practice of second-wave feminism. Women who defined themselves as lesbians before the late 1960s initially had an uneasy relationship with the new feminist movement, which many saw as homophobic (not without reason: one of its leading figures, Betty Friedan, described lesbians as a 'lavender menace' whose presence in the movement would undermine mainstream support for its objectives). Some lesbians continued to feel that the Gay Liberation movement was more relevant to their concerns; others, however, became a visible and radical presence within the Women's

Liberation Movement. Involvement in feminist groups also led some women who had previously thought of themselves as heterosexual to discover the erotic potential of relationships between women, and to redefine themselves as lesbians. Today it is widely assumed that individuals do not choose, and cannot change, their sexual preferences, but in the past, feminists tended to see sexuality as more plastic. The fact that a married woman came out as a lesbian in her thirties (or her sixties) did not necessarily mean that she had always been a lesbian but was previously unaware of it or unable to admit it. That was one possibility, but it was also possible for identities and desires to change in response to new experiences, particularly during times of significant social and cultural change.

The present is arguably another time in which identities and desires are being reshaped by new social and cultural developments. One indication of this shift, it has been suggested, is that young women are turning away from lesbianism, and towards what they see as the more inclusive or fluid identity that is designated by the term 'queer'. 'Queer' was once a common insult meaning 'homosexual', but in the 'reclaimed' usage that emerged from the queer theory and activism of the 1980s and 1990s, it does not refer exclusively to gay men and lesbians. Rather, it includes all sexual preferences and practices that challenge 'heteronormativity', a term which denotes the social privileging of a particular form of heterosexuality – monogamous, procreative, involving traditional gender roles and conventional erotic practices. So, if more women are indeed defining themselves as 'queer' rather than 'lesbian', the question arises of whether this is just a shift in terminology (they're still doing the same things with the same people, but under a different label), or whether it is a sign of more far-reaching changes in the social organisation of sexuality. This is a complicated question, but one answer is hinted at by the commentator who observed that 'against the increasingly colorful backdrop of gender diversity, a binary label like "gay" or "lesbian" starts to feel somewhat stale and stodgy'. Current shifts in our ways of talking, thinking about and perhaps also having sex are closely connected to changing ideas about gender identity – a subject I'll return to in the final chapter.

Meanwhile, since this chapter has had so much to say about the divisions among feminists on the subject of sex, I will conclude by saying something about what unites them – what makes all the views I have been considering, however different they are from one another, 'feminist'. Put briefly, it is the assertion that women are, and should be treated as, autonomous sexual subjects, not objects to be used for others' pleasure and profit. Women should be free to express their sexuality, without being reduced to it or defined exclusively in sexual terms. Their desires should matter, and their boundaries should be respected. As basic as these demands might seem, they are radical demands even now.

6

CULTURE

In 1990 the critic Camille Paglia declared that 'if civilization had been left in female hands, we would still be living in grass huts'. This was not an original thought. Paglia was recycling the old idea that men are the creators of culture (using that word not in its anthropological sense of 'a whole way of life', but as an umbrella term for the most valued products of human intellect and creativity), because of their drive to transcend and control the forces of nature. Women, meanwhile, remain tethered to nature, using their creative energies not in the pursuit of knowledge, truth and beauty, but in the natural process of reproduction.

In *The Descent of Man*, his major work on human evolution, Charles Darwin pondered the evidence of women's cultural inferiority. 'If two lists were made of the most eminent men and women in poetry, painting, sculpture, music, history, science and philosophy,' he mused, 'the two lists would not bear comparison.' He concluded that the difference must have a biological cause: men were innately endowed with 'a higher standard of mental power'. That was also the view of Cesare Lombroso, the nineteenth-century Italian physician and criminologist who published a book-length study entitled *L'Uomo di Genio* ('The Man of Genius'). This text includes a section on 'the influence of sex', which begins by observing that 'in the history of genius women have but a small place'. On the next page we discover that even this is an overstatement: the few female candidates for the title of genius all turn out to have 'something virile about them'. Lombroso concludes that 'there are no women of genius: the women of genius are men.'

Absurd though we may find this logic, the basic argument remains a cliché of popular anti-feminism. If women are really men's equals, people say, where is the female Leonardo/ Shakespeare/ Mozart? Which woman philosopher or political thinker has had the influence of Confucius, Plato or Marx? Why are there so few female Nobel laureates, and how do we explain the fact that only one woman (the late Maryam Mirzakhani) has ever won the prestigious Fields Medal for mathematics?

The anti-feminist tradition to which these questions belong is a very old one (in the introduction I mentioned one early attempt to defend women against the charge of all-round inferiority, Christine de Pizan's *The Book of the City of Ladies*). In this chapter I will consider some of the answers that feminists have given, and more generally how they have theorised women's relationship to art, knowledge and creativity since the nineteenth century. (I should acknowledge here that this discussion will have a strong focus on Western and European traditions: these are not, of course, the only traditions of interest, and feminist accounts of women's place within them should not be taken – even if they have sometimes been presented – as universal statements about the relationship of all women to all cultural traditions.)

The first-wave feminists who were Darwin's contemporaries did not generally dispute that women's intellectual and artistic achievements were fewer and less distinguished than those of 'the most eminent men'. What they did dispute, however, was that this state of affairs was immutable. Many feminists were enthusiastic supporters of Darwin, because the idea that every species developed through a continuous process of adaptation seemed to support their belief that women, if given the opportunity, were capable of developing to the same level as men. Faced with his disparaging comments in *The Descent of Man*, the American feminist Antoinette Brown Blackwell accused Darwin of failing to follow his own logic. 'The difference of sex', she wrote, 'whatever it may consist in, must itself be subject to natural selection and to evolution.'

Whether or not they used arguments drawn from evolutionary theory, feminists in the nineteenth and early twentieth centuries were in no doubt that women's contributions to culture had been limited by their subordinate status, their lack of education and their confinement to the domestic sphere. In *A Room of One's Own*, Virginia Woolf addresses the perennial 'why no female Shakespeare' question by asking whether a hypothetical Judith Shakespeare, William's equally gifted sister, could have risen to the same heights as her brother in the conditions of early modern England. The life story she constructs for the fictional Judith makes clear that the answer must be 'no'. Unlike William, Judith is never sent to school: she does learn to read, but if her mother sees her reading she is scolded for neglecting her domestic chores. When she is seventeen her parents decide that it's time to find her a husband, and she is betrothed to a local wool-stapler. Horrified by the prospect of marriage, she runs away to London to seek her fortune in the theatre. But the Elizabethan theatre does not employ women, and the city is a dangerous place for a young woman on her own. Eventually Judith finds a male patron, but – predictably – his support has a price. Unmarried and pregnant, she takes her own life.

In Woolf's own time, the early twentieth century, women of her class had more opportunity than Shakespeare's sister to develop their talents, but they were still not in the same position as their brothers. *A Room of One's Own* discusses a number of obstacles that stood in their way: inferior education, economic dependence, the continuing expectation that they would put their roles as wives and mothers first. For less privileged women, the barriers were much higher. In her 1974 essay 'In search of our mothers' gardens', Alice Walker asks: 'What did it mean for a Black woman to be an artist in our grandmothers' time?', adding: 'It is a question with an answer cruel enough to stop the blood.' Yet as she goes on to point out, poor and uneducated Black women did not lack creativity. The talents which might, in other conditions, have produced great literature or painting or sculpture were channelled instead into oral storytelling, quilt-making or, in Walker's mother's case, the gardens of the essay's title.

Today, women are told that they can do anything they put their minds to, and be judged entirely on their merits; but in practice the proverbial playing field is far from level. In a 2017 lecture on women and film (entitled, in homage to Woolf, 'A screen of one's own'), the director Susanna White looked back on her own career, retracing a route that had been full of obstacles, detours and dead ends – though at least she ended up at her chosen destination, which many women in her profession still do not. For the past fifteen years, equal numbers of women and men have been graduating from film school with ambitions to become feature film directors. But of those who go on to achieve their goal, the vast majority are men. In Britain in 2016, men directed six times as many films as women. Most of the films women do direct are modest, low-budget productions: only 3 per cent of big-budget films are made by a woman director. White believes that the imbalance reflects ingrained sexist assumptions that are difficult to challenge because they are rarely made explicit. For instance, it is assumed that women will find it harder to manage a large cast and crew, and that those who have families will be unwilling to work long hours (though some of the longest hours on film sets are worked by people in the costume, hair and make-up departments, which have always been dominated by women). Another common assumption is that women can only direct certain kinds of material, like children's films and domestic dramas. White was offered her own first feature after she had been nominated for an Emmy for her work on a TV mini-series about the invasion of Iraq. Nevertheless, what she was offered was a film for children. (She imagined the voice-over on the trailer: 'From the director of *Generation Kill*: *Nanny McPhee and the Big Bang*.') She has since directed a big-budget thriller and a historical drama. But as she says, this is very unusual: in mainstream cinema it is so rare for women directors to be able to compile a sizeable body of work that most people can't even name more than a handful of them (Kathryn Bigelow, Jane Campion, Sophia Coppola …).

Will those names be remembered a hundred years from now? We might hope so, but another form of cultural exclusion that feminists have documented is the persistent tendency for women, even those whose talents were recognised in their own time, to be erased from the historical record. In 1970 Shulamith Firestone could answer her own question, 'What about the women who have contributed directly to culture?' with a brief: 'There aren't many.' But feminist scholarship would subsequently reveal that there had been more than Firestone knew. Documenting women's past cultural contributions became (and is still) an important goal for feminist research: it matters not only because of the intrinsic value of the work it brings to light, but also because making women's achievements visible challenges the belief that 'there have never been any great women Xs' – a belief about the past which continues to discourage and exclude women in the present.

In the realm of science, feminist scholarship has called attention to women such as Caroline Herschel (an eighteenth-century German-born astronomer who was the first woman to be made an (honorary) member of the Royal Society), Mary Anning (the fossil collector and palaeontologist), Ada Lovelace (a pioneer in the development of computing), Nettie Stevens (the US biologist who, in 1905, identified the role of the X and Y chromosomes in sex determination), Lise Meitner (the mid-twentieth-century Austrian nuclear physicist who was the co-discoverer, with Otto Hahn, of nuclear fission), Jocelyn Bell Burnell (an astrophysicist who, as a PhD student in the 1960s, discovered pulsars), and Katherine Johnson (the NASA mathematician whose story was told in the 2016 film *Hidden Figures*). And in a field of artistic endeavour whose canonical figures are almost without exception male – musical composition in the Western classical tradition – scholarship has revealed a wealth of female talent going back centuries. In her book *Sounds and Sweet Airs: The Forgotten Women of Classical Music*, Anna Beer discusses not only some women whose names we know because of their connection to a famous male composer (like Mendelssohn's sister Fanny Hensel, and Clara Wieck, who married Schumann), but also numerous less familiar examples, like Francesca Caccini, who worked as a court composer in Renaissance Florence, Elisabeth Jacquet de la Guerre, the first Frenchwoman to have an opera performed (in Paris in 1694), and Marianna Martines, a compatriot and contemporary of Haydn who in her own lifetime was highly regarded as a composer of sacred music.

In addition to writing these women back into the record, feminists have asked how they came to be erased. In the case of the scientists, a recurring theme is 'the Matilda effect', a tendency to credit women's achievements to the men they work with (it is named after the US suffragist Matilda Joslyn Gage, who wrote about the phenomenon in the late nineteenth century). Neither Lise Meitner nor Jocelyn Bell Burnell was honoured with a Nobel prize – not because their discoveries were overlooked, but because in each case the Nobel committee chose to award the prize to a man (Meitner's collaborator Otto Hahn, and Bell Burnell's

PhD supervisor). Even Marie Curie, the one woman scientist almost everyone can name, was initially left out of the nomination for the 1903 Nobel prize that she ultimately shared with Henri Becquerel and her husband Pierre – she was added only after Pierre complained. The committees in these cases apparently could not imagine a male–female partnership in which the woman was an equal partner (let alone one in which she took the lead). This problem is not confined to science: Anna Beer mentions the case of Rebecca Clarke, who was awarded a prize in 1919 for a violin sonata she had composed – only for questions to be asked about whether she had, in fact, composed it, or whether it might have been submitted by a man using a female pseudonym. It was even suggested that the man in question might be the French composer Maurice Ravel – a compliment to Clarke's abilities, but an insult to her sex. ('There are no women of genius: the women of genius are men.')

In the arts, a common way of devaluing women's work is to relegate it to the category of the 'minor' – to say, yes, some of these women are competent, but they do not rise to the level of greatness: their work is mediocre, derivative, trivial, sentimental, 'light'. It has, in other words, the same negative qualities that are often attributed to women themselves. This trope was identified by feminists early on. In 1968 the literary critic Mary Ellmann complained that 'books by women are treated as though they themselves were women, and criticism embarks ... upon an intellectual measuring of busts and hips.' It still seems to be impossible for women writers *not* to be read through the prism of gender, as the novelist Catherine Nichols discovered in 2015 when, as an experiment, she sent the same manuscript out to literary agents using either her own name or the name of a fictitious male alter ego. The agents who read Catherine's work praised her 'lyrical' writing; those who thought they were reading the work of 'George', on the other hand, commended his prose for being 'clever' and 'well-constructed'. It was George whose writing the agents preferred. With seventeen expressions of interest to Catherine's two, George was, as Nichols drily remarked, 'eight and a half times more successful than me at writing the same book'.

Since in reality all the agents had read the same text, their more positive response to 'George' suggests that their judgements were affected by an unconscious bias towards men. Sexism can also, of course, be conscious and deliberate. Either way, it is one very basic reason why women's work is so persistently judged inferior or 'minor'. Another is that women have often been restricted to less prestigious forms and genres. Women composers in the past were rarely able to compose symphonic works for large orchestras; women painters were often commissioned or expected to paint 'female' subjects, like the domestic interiors and mother-and-child portraits which we associate with the Impressionists Berthe Morisot and Mary Cassatt. There is also the question of what is preserved for posterity. Francesca Caccini will always remain a little-known, minor figure, because her scores have not survived to be performed and studied. And in the visual arts, as the anonymous feminist activists who call themselves 'Guerrilla Girls' have been pointing out since 1985, women's work is devalued and rendered 'minor' by its absence or under-representation in museum collections and exhibitions. One famous Guerrilla Girl poster asked: 'Do women have to be naked to get into the Met. Museum?' It pointed out that in the New York City Metropolitan Museum, works by women artists are massively outnumbered by works depicting naked women.

No feminist would dispute that women artists, writers, musicians and film-makers deserve the same opportunities and the same recognition as their male counterparts. But some would argue that giving a few exceptional women their place in a tradition or canon that has unjustly excluded them does not address the deeper problem, which is the male-centredness of culture itself. The standards we use to judge 'greatness', or 'merit', or even what counts as art or knowledge in the first place, are not neutral standards: they belong to a cultural tradition created by men, for men, and in the image of men. As Simone de Beauvoir put it, 'men describe [the world] from their own point of view, which they confuse with absolute truth.' That's why feminists should care who holds the pen, the brush or the camera: it is not just a question of demanding equal opportunities for individual artists who happen to be female, but also a matter of wanting the world to be represented from a different point of view, in a way that challenges patriarchal assumptions and standards.

While she acknowledges that neither women nor men share a single point of view, Susanna White argues in 'A screen of one's own' that there are nevertheless differences, stemming from their different social positions and life experiences, in the way that men and women relate to the world, and therefore in the stories they can tell about it. If 'the screens we watch mirror our society back at us', then we should worry about what is not being reflected – or what is being distorted – when all the stories are told by men. The way we see ourselves represented in art influences our perceptions of what is possible and desirable in life – a point White illustrates by citing the first *Hunger Games* film, in which the female protagonist, Katniss, is highly skilled with a bow and arrow. This prompted a huge increase in the number of girls taking up archery. The particular example might be trivial, but the general principle is not.

Can it really be assumed, though, that simply increasing the number of representations made by women will automatically produce a different picture? Hasn't everyone's way of seeing the world, women's as well as men's, been shaped by patriarchal traditions? Shulamith Firestone believed so. Discussing the work of some nineteenth-century women painters, she remarked that 'they saw women through male eyes, painted a male's idea of female.' For Firestone, the necessity of working in a tradition created by men rendered the art made by these women 'inauthentic', but at the same time she recognised that it *was* a necessity: no alternative, authentically female tradition existed. In the years after she wrote, a number of theorists and art practitioners would explore this issue in greater depth. How are women brought to see themselves and the world 'through male eyes'? Could feminists create new traditions and, if so, what would their representations look like?

In his 1972 book *Ways of Seeing*, based on a TV series with the same title, John Berger considered how the conventions of Western representational art have both reflected and reinforced patriarchal assumptions about women's nature and social role. The most famous part of his discussion explains that in both life and art:

> *Men act and women appear.* Men look at women. Women watch themselves being looked at. This determines not only most relations between men and women, but also women's relation to themselves. The surveyor of woman in herself is male: the surveyed female. Thus she turns herself into an object – and most particularly an object of vision: a sight.

Berger illustrates this thesis with a discussion of the European tradition of nude painting. The female nude, he explains, is an object of erotic desire for a spectator who is assumed to be a heterosexual male. But in many cases the artist represents her in a way that makes her complicit in, if not responsible for, her own objectification. He might paint her with her body twisted towards the spectator, its unnatural contortion underlining her eagerness to display herself; he might paint her looking straight at the spectator, actively soliciting and taking pleasure in his desire; or he might show her admiring herself in a mirror. (Berger finds this especially hypocritical: 'You put a mirror in her hand and called the painting "Vanity", thus morally condemning the woman whose nakedness you had depicted for your own pleasure.') The woman's body is a commodity in a transaction between men – the one who paints her and the one(s) who paid for her to be painted – but the conventions for representing her make it seem as if she is in control.

Three years after *Ways of Seeing*, the feminist film-maker and theorist Laura Mulvey published an academic article entitled 'Visual pleasure and narrative cinema', in which she elaborated the concept of the 'male gaze'. This phrase is now often used to mean simply 'the way men look at women', but Mulvey was talking about something more complicated. Like Berger, she argued that the conventions of representation – in this case specifically those of mainstream narrative cinema – call on the spectator, whoever he or she may be, to adopt the viewpoint of a (heterosexual) man: to identify with the male protagonist(s) who are at the centre of the action, and to look at the female characters in the same (typically objectifying) way they are looked at by the men on screen. In the case of film, one key instrument for achieving this effect – making the audience look *with* the male characters and *at* the female ones – is the camera. What viewers see or pay attention to is constrained by the positioning and the movement of the camera (though in realist cinema film-makers will usually try to minimise viewers' awareness of this), and these choices are typically made in such a way as to align the camera, and thus the viewer's gaze, with the male protagonist's point of view. For instance, the camera might show a male character looking intently at a woman, thus encouraging viewers to look with him, or it might communicate that he is looking at her by mimicking the trajectory of his gaze – panning slowly over the female character's body, say, or zooming in to show parts of her in close-up. The 'male gaze' thus becomes the default way of looking, not just for heterosexual men but for all viewers. And this highly gendered way of looking becomes associated with the pleasure we get from the whole experience of watching films. This is another way in which women as well as men are induced to objectify the female body.

More recent work from a Black and/or intersectional feminist perspective has emphasised that the gaze which is constructed in Western/European art is not only male, but also white, racist and colonialist. Directed towards Black women, this gaze produces a distinctive form of objectification. A number of writers have examined how this worked in the case of Sarah Baartman, a Khoisan woman who was taken from South Africa to Europe in the early nineteenth century to be exhibited to paying audiences under the racist soubriquet 'The Hottentot Venus'. Not only in life but even after her death, when for the benefit of European 'race science' her body was dissected and parts of it displayed in a museum, Baartman was literally treated as a specimen, an exemplar of the 'primitive' and hypersexual African woman. She was not viewed as, in T. Denean Sharpley-Whiting's words, 'a person, or even a human, but rather a titillating curiosity, a collage of buttocks and genitalia'. And while few Europeans today would defend this treatment, some continue to make use of the degrading iconography found in nineteenth-century images of Black women like Baartman. Those images are clearly alluded to, for instance, in Jean-Paul Goude's famous photograph of Grace Jones naked and on all fours in a cage and, more recently, of Kim Kardashian balancing a champagne glass on her buttocks (though Kardashian, who is white, wears an evening dress and gloves).

Theoretical accounts like the ones I have been discussing are intended, in the first instance, to explain how certain representations work and what they accomplish in the process. But they may also prompt experiments with alternative forms of representation. Laura Mulvey advocated (and produced, with her collaborator Peter Wollen), a kind of cinema that did not rely on the conventions she had criticised, but required the viewer to adopt a more detached position, and to be aware of the camera as a material presence. Other feminist film-makers have challenged the conventions of mainstream cinema in other ways. In the Belgian director Chantal Akerman's film *Jeanne Dielman, 23 Quai du Commerce, 1080 Bruxelles* (made in the same year that Mulvey's essay was published, and hailed by the *New York Times* as 'the first masterpiece of the feminine in the history of the cinema') the eponymous protagonist, a single mother who supports herself and her son by selling sex to male clients in her home, is shown going about her daily routine over a period of three consecutive days. Mundane activities like making beds, washing dishes and preparing meals are shot in real time, disrupting the usual expectation that dramatic or unexpected events will be foregrounded, while monotonous or routine ones will remain unseen or in the background (a convention which, as Akerman has pointed out, renders much of what most women spend their time on invisible). Jeanne's sex work is accorded no more importance than her housework, and neither is glamourised in any way. Something dramatic does eventually happen (which I won't describe, because it's worth watching the film for yourself), but Akerman resolutely resists treating any part of the narrative, such as it is, in the conventional Hollywood manner.

At the end of her essay on visual pleasure Laura Mulvey acknowledged that 1970s radical film-making denied audiences the kind of pleasure and satisfaction they got from conventional narrative cinema. But she evidently considered that no great loss. 'Women', she concluded, 'whose image has continually been stolen and used for that end [i.e. satisfying the demands of the male gaze] cannot view the decline of the traditional film form with much more than sentimental regret.' We might wonder, though, how many women outside film theory and art cinema would agree. More than 40 years on, it is evident that the 'traditional film form' has not become obsolete: if what's showing at my local multiplex is any guide, most people who watch films are still wedded to the pleasures of narrative cinema. That is not to say that feminists *shouldn't* make art which radically challenges the audience's expectations, but it might suggest that less radical interventions are needed too. In a society where sexist representations remain entrenched and all-pervasive, changes of the kind Susanna White discusses (e.g. more women behind the camera, more leading and speaking roles for women in front of it, more diversity in the stories told on film) could also make a positive difference.

I have called these 'less radical interventions', but in recent years it has often seemed as if any kind of feminist intervention is considered intolerably radical. Consider, for instance, how much outrage was generated by the 2016 remake of the popular Hollywood film *Ghostbusters,* which cast four women in the lead roles originally played by men. Or think back to 2013, when the Bank of England announced that a banknote featuring the Quaker social reformer Elizabeth Fry would be replaced with a new one depicting Winston Churchill. Realising what this meant – that by 2016, all four of the English banknotes in circulation would carry images of men – the writer and activist Caroline Criado-Perez started a campaign for the next historical figure pictured on a banknote to be female. She was promptly deluged with rape and death threats, some of them so serious that the people responsible received prison sentences. And in 2012 the US-based media critic Anita Sarkeesian became the target of a prolonged campaign of harassment (one of her harassers made a video game called 'Beat up Anita Sarkeesian'; another threatened to shoot her at a lecture she was scheduled to deliver). What had Sarkeesian done to provoke this reaction? The answer is, she had made a series of videos called *Tropes vs. Women*, in which she analysed examples of sexism in video games.

In each of these cases, the response seems out of all proportion to whatever precipitated it. Why were so many people so threatened by the idea that there might be room in the world for *one* banknote depicting a woman, or *one* mainstream film in which women played all the main roles? Perhaps the intensity of the anger speaks not only to the conviction that culture is or should be a male preserve, but also to the centrality of cultural issues in contemporary sexual politics. Today's most prominent anti-feminist ideologues, the 'meninists' of the alt-right, put most of their energy into cultural politics: they believe that culture change is a necessary condition for political change, rather than vice versa. Both feminists and anti-feminists have always understood that the cultural is political: ideas, images,

stories and theories play an important part in sustaining –
or challenging – inequality. What the alt-right has been able
to harness in recent years is the feeling among many men in
Western democracies that cultural privilege is the only kind
they have left. It's easy to mock this ('we've let women be
fighter pilots/ professional footballers/ prime ministers, but
NO WAY are we going to let them be ghostbusters!'), but
the resentment is real, and its consequences can be serious.
For feminists this is not a new battleground, but we should
not underestimate its current and future importance.

7

FAULTLINES AND FUTURES

Attempts to summarise the current state of feminism crop up regularly: *Prospect* magazine published one in 2017 under the heading 'Everything you ever wanted to know about fourth wave feminism – but were afraid to ask'. 'New breadth', it said, 'has made it harder to define a coherent feminism for the 21st century'. If 'coherent' means 'unified in its ideas and political goals', then it isn't obvious that today's feminism is less coherent than what preceded it; hindsight often makes the past look more coherent than it felt to the people for whom it was the present. But it could be argued that a kind of coherence is now being imposed from the outside, as feminists confront the challenges of the current political situation.

Since the 2008 financial crisis, the situation of women in many places has worsened both economically, because of the impact of government austerity programmes, and politically, because of a resurgence of nationalism and right-wing authoritarianism. In countries as different as India, Poland, Russia, Turkey and the US (this is not a full list), authoritarian leaders and conservative lawmakers are making efforts to reverse the gains of the recent past (in Poland they tried to ban abortion completely; in Russia they have decriminalised many forms of domestic violence). In some places feminists are being harassed by agents of the state: Human Rights Watch reported in 2017 that a group of Russian women attending a feminist event had been interrogated by the police and warned about their 'extremist activities'. In other places, it is far-right groups who are doing the harassing. In the US, analysts of the alt-right have found a strong connection between involvement in neo-Nazi or white supremacist organisations and engagement in men's rights activism. In these conditions the political agenda becomes all too clear: 'fight back'. Coherence is not always a good sign.

Effective resistance requires a broad-based coalition in which diverse constituencies and voices are represented. For feminists, that underlines, once again, the necessity of acknowledging and addressing relations of power and inequality among women. In principle this is something that feminists agree on. The *Prospect* article is not the first to suggest that commitment to the principle of intersectionality is one of the defining features of the 'fourth wave'. But it is one thing to talk the intersectional talk, and another to walk the walk. The Women's Marches that were organised to protest Donald Trump's inauguration were on one level an impressive display of feminist unity, but they were also the site of conflicts about the exclusion or marginalisation of some groups of women by others. Black women pointed out that the original organisers were all white, and that the names they chose for the event were borrowed, without acknowledgement, from earlier Black women's and civil rights protests. One activist told the organisers in an open letter why she could not support the march: 'Politically co-opting efforts with "ALL WOMEN" and "ALL VOICES" is merely an attempt to erase the specific needs of people of African descent.' There was also some debate on whether the signature 'pussy hats' and 'pussy power' signs (references to the infamous tape on which Trump was heard boasting about 'grabbing women by the pussy') were exclusionary and disrespectful to trans women.

The fact that this became an issue points to another characteristic of the 'fourth wave': its concern with new questions about gender identity and diversity. For most of its history, feminism has been understood (and often referred to) as a 'women's movement', a movement which seeks rights, equality or liberation for women as a class. To complain, as Laurie Penny did in 2015, that 'feminism's focus on women can be alienating' would have been rather like complaining that a baker's shop sold bread (or else it would have suggested that you were the kind of anti-feminist whose refrain throughout the ages has been 'but what about the men?'). Today, however, there is a significant constituency within feminism which is questioning the basis for the traditional definition.

Laurie Penny belongs to a new wave of 'genderqueer' activists who conceive of feminism not simply as a movement to end the oppression of women and the dominance of men, but as a movement to liberate everyone from the rigid binary gender system that produces these two categories in the first place. Like many other people who define themselves as something other than 'men' or 'women' – trans, non-binary, agender, genderfluid, (gender)queer – Penny recalls feeling from an early age that the standard binary categories were inadequate to capture her own sense of who she was (though she has continued to define herself as a woman, and would not object to my use of the pronoun *she*). From this perspective, gender is not seen in the way that second-wave feminists saw it, as a set of restrictive and unequal roles imposed by societies on their male and female members, but rather as a form of identity which individuals should be free to define for themselves. Whereas second-wave feminists often imagined, both in their political writings and in utopian fiction, a future world without gender distinctions (one where, as Shulamith Firestone put it in 1970, 'genital differences would no longer matter culturally'), Penny has a different vision:

> I don't want to see a world without gender. I want to see a world where gender is not oppressive or enforced, where there are as many ways to express and perform and relate to your own identity as there are people on Earth. I want a world where gender is not painful, but joyful.

It could be argued that this isn't, in the end, so very different from what the 'gender critical' feminists who follow in Firestone's footsteps want to see. If there really were as many gender identities as there were people on the planet, then gender in its present form would effectively have ceased to exist: the word would no longer mean 'a social role imposed on the basis of a person's sex', but something more like 'a set of behaviours that express an individual's personality'. If genderqueer feminism and the descendant of Firestone's radical feminism are just different routes to the same destination, why is there a conflict between them?

One answer is that while virtually all feminists agree

that gender is socially constructed, they have differing ideas about what it is constructed for, and whose interests it serves for it to be constructed in the ways that it is. As I explained in chapter 4, it can be argued that the qualities and behaviours that a culture codes as 'feminine' or 'masculine' are not just arbitrarily different: they are designed to justify men's dominance while keeping women in their subordinate place. Feminists who see gender in this way are sceptical about the idea that self-conscious or ironic gender 'performances' (a concept drawn from the work of the feminist/queer theorist Judith Butler), are politically subversive. As Laurie Penny notes (though she herself does not agree), some feminists feel that queer and trans performances, especially if they involve performing a stereotypical version of femininity or masculinity, do not subvert but rather reinforce the system which subordinates women to men.

Another answer is that contemporary gender identity politics raises fundamental questions about what defines the category 'women', and this is also something on which feminists have differing views. Though many or most of them subscribe to the belief that 'one is not born, but rather becomes, a woman', the question can still be asked: how does one become a woman? Can anyone become a woman, or does it require a certain kind of personal history (of being treated, from birth, in the way your culture treats girls, as opposed to the way it treats boys)? Are there aspects of becoming a woman that are inextricably connected to having a certain kind of body? Even if we acknowledge that bodies exist in a social context which profoundly shapes the experience of embodiment, are there material bodily realities that will always be relevant to the feminist project of ending women's oppression?

Laurie Penny believes that the (traditional) feminist project and genderqueer feminism are not incompatible: she says that 'sex is also a political category, and politically, I'm still on the girls' team'. However, other feminists (on both sides) are less sure that the two perspectives can be reconciled. This has become a high-profile and very polarised debate, but it is also a fast-moving one: how it will develop even in the short term is hard to predict. The conflict it has generated is often presented as primarily generational (i.e. critics of the new gender identity politics are said to be older feminists whose ideas were formed by the second wave, and whose perspective will inevitably become less and less relevant as feminism comes to be dominated by younger women who think differently), but arguably this is another case of something I mentioned in the introduction, the tendency of the 'wave' model of feminism to flatten out the political differences that exist within each generational cohort. Different and conflicting views about the nature and meaning of gender go along with differing ideas about what feminism is and what it is for, and those differences will be part of feminism's future just as they are part of its present, and of its history.

The prominence of gender identity as an issue in contemporary feminism speaks to a more general cultural preoccupation with identity in all its forms, and recently this has prompted some critical reflections on the state of feminism today. Sylvia Walby observes that in the twenty-first century feminism itself has increasingly come to be conceptualised as a kind of personal identity rather than as a political project: we ask '*is* person X a feminist?' rather than 'does person X *do* feminism?' This emphasis on self-definition, Walby says, can work against the goals of intersectionality and inclusion, since it does not recognise as 'feminist' projects that are, in fact, doing feminism – resisting women's oppression and working for women's advancement – but which involve individuals and organisations (such as trades unions) that do not define themselves primarily in terms of feminism. Precisely because these projects centre on the intersections of gender with race and class, their invisibility or non-recognition as feminist projects results in the marginalisation of working-class, Black and minority ethnic feminists.

Some commentators have linked the rise of feminism-as-identity to the way consumer capitalism appropriates images and ideas from grassroots movements and makes them into marketable commodities. In her book *We Were Feminists Once,* Andi Zeisler argues that feminism is now being promoted as 'an identity that everyone can and should consume', and that the result is to dilute and depoliticise it. People who may have no commitment to any concrete polit-ical project are being encouraged to claim a feminist identity simply by purchasing products which symbolise feminism. An example turned up in my Facebook feed recently: it was an advertisement for a product called FeministBox™. Priced at over £50, the box contained a T-shirt, a tote bag, a badge, some stickers, a book and two zines – plus a coupon which gave the recipient a discount on the company's other products. In 2017, fashion-conscious consumers with enough disposable cash could also consider purchasing, for $710 (with a percentage of the proceeds going to a charity founded by Rihanna), Dior's limited edition T-shirt emblazoned with the words 'We should all be feminists'.

Another criticism that has been made of this commodified version of feminism is that it reduces political questions to matters of personal choice, producing the sort of vacuous discourse parodied in the satirical newspaper *The Onion*, which once marked International Women's Day with a story headed 'Women now empowered by anything a woman does'. Arguments about whether feminism is first and foremost a politics of individual choice can arise in relation to highly consequential political issues (such as whether and how to reform the law on abortion, or prostitution), but often they are sparked by less momentous questions. For instance, when the writer Zadie Smith told a newspaper in 2017 that she worried about girls spending too much time on beauty and make-up routines, adding that she limited her own daughter's mirror-time to fifteen minutes a day, some feminists accused her of attacking women who chose to wear make-up; it was also suggested that she had no business voicing an opinion because she herself was too beautiful to need cosmetic enhancement.

As Smith's defenders pointed out, what she was really criticising was the societal pressure put on women and girls to pay so much attention to their looks. As I noted in chapter 4, women's decisions about things like wearing make-up are influenced by their understanding that conforming or not conforming to prevailing beauty standards has material consequences; they will also be influenced by feelings and desires which are produced by the way girls are socialised. One implication of 'the personal is political' is that we cannot think of our individual choices as entirely 'free', since they are always shaped by the context in which they are made. And as current debates on identity and choice suggest, the same applies to feminism itself.

Feminism may be having one of its periodic moments of being 'on trend', but the message of writers like Andi Zeisler is that being a feminist, in the sense that requires more than just buying the T-shirt, is not easy or undemanding. Why do feminists do it? When I put that question to a group of feminist women, their answers focused not on the difficulties and sacrifices that political activism entailed, but on the way it had enriched their own lives. Feminism, they said, had given them a new understanding of the world which had helped them to make sense of their own experiences; it had enabled them to connect in positive ways with other women, and made them more rather than less convinced that radical change was possible. Many spoke of the relief they felt when they discovered a community of women who felt the same dissatisfactions they had believed they were alone in feeling. 'It saved my sanity', said one; another said, 'it changed my life'. Their relationships with these other feminist women (as one put it, 'badass women who are not afraid to think for themselves'), were important to all of them. And while they had all had to deal with political conflicts and setbacks, they were positive about the future. 'Feminism offers optimism. It gives the opportunity to create change.'

Whatever the challenges facing feminism today, I think

this optimism is justified. The basic principles of feminism have achieved global currency: their influence is felt in some way in virtually all contemporary societies, including those which still deny women basic rights and freedoms. Though it will continue to be resisted in some quarters, and to provoke arguments about what follows from it in practice, 'the radical notion that women are people' is not going to go away.

REFERENCES

Here is a chronological list of some key theoretical texts which are referred to in this book:

Christine de Pizan, *The Book of the City of Ladies* [c. 1400] (Penguin Books, 1999)

Mary Wollstonecraft, *A Vindication of the Rights of Woman* [1792] (Penguin Books, 2004)

Friedrich Engels, *The Origins of the Family, Private Property and the State*, 4th edn, 1891, https://www.marxists.org/archive/marx/works/download/pdf/origin_family.pdf

Margaret Mead, *Sex and Temperament in Three Primitive Societies* [1935] (HarperCollins, 2001)

Simone de Beauvoir, *The Second Sex* [1949], trans. Constance Borde and Sheila Malovany-Chevallier (Knopf, 2009)

Shulamith Firestone, *The Dialectic of Sex* [1970] (Verso, 2015)

Angela Davis, *Women, Race and Class* (Vintage, 1983)

bell hooks, *Feminist Theory: From Margin to Center* (South End Press, 1984)

Gerda Lerner, *The Creation of Patriarchy* (Oxford University Press, 1986)

Judith Butler, *Gender Trouble: Feminism and the Subversion of Identity* (Routledge, 1990)

Sylvia Walby, *Theorising Patriarchy* (Blackwell, 1990)

FURTHER INVESTIGATIONS

INTRODUCTION

Two recent books presenting feminism for a general audience are Chimamanda Ngozi Adichie, *We Should All Be Feminists* (Fourth Estate, 2014) and bell hooks, *Feminism is for Everybody: Passionate Politics*, 2nd edn. (Routledge, 2015).

The text of Dorothy Sayers's lecture 'Are women human?' is included in a collection of her essays, *Unpopular Opinions* (Gollancz, 1946). The quotation from Winifred Holtby on p. 1 comes from her book *Women and a Changing Civilisation* (John Lane, 1934). For a short overview of the women's movement in Britain between 1850 and 1939, see http://www.historytoday.com/martin-pugh/womens-movement. A concise history of US feminism from 1920 to the present is Dorothy Sue Cobble, Linda Gordon and Astrid Henry, *Feminism Unfinished* (Norton, 2014). Heidi Safia Mirza's edited volume *British Black Feminism: A Reader* (Routledge, 1997) contains a good selection of twentieth-century theoretical and political writings by British Black feminists and feminists of colour, while Julia Sudbury's '*Other Kinds of Dreams*' (Routledge, 1998) is a history of Black British women's political organising.

Kimberlé Crenshaw discusses intersectionality at http://www.ted.com/talks/kimberle_crenshaw_the_urgency_of_intersectionality. A useful short introduction to the subject is Patricia Hill Collins and Sirma Bilge, *Intersectionality* (Polity Press, 2016).

On feminism as a global movement, see Amrita Basu, ed., *Women's Movements in the Global Era* (Routledge, 2016).

1. DOMINATION

For more on speculative fiction as a vehicle for exploring feminist theoretical ideas, see Judith A. Little, ed., *Feminist Philosophy and Science Fiction: Utopias and Dystopias* (Prometheus Books, 2007). The fictional texts referenced in this chapter are Naomi Alderman, *The Power* (Penguin, 2016); Marge Piercy, *Woman on the Edge of Time* (Women's Press, 1976); and Charlotte Perkins Gilman, *Herland* [1915] (Vintage Classics, 2015).

2. RIGHTS

On women's rights around the world, the UN Women's website offers facts, figures and links to UN documents: http://www.unwomen.org/en/what-we-do. Catharine MacKinnon's book *Are Women Human?* (Harvard University Press, 2006) contains a selection of her writings on women, law and human rights. Charlotte Bunch talks about her work as an activist at http://www..com/charlotte-bunch.

One classic feminist treatment of reproductive rights is Angela Davis's chapter on birth control and sterilisation abuse in *Women, Race and Class*. On the contemporary politics of abortion, see Katha Pollitt, *Pro: Reclaiming Abortion Rights* (Picador, 2014).

On minority and religious rights, see Christine Delphy, *Separate and Dominate* (Verso, 2015) and Yasmin Rehman's review of Delphy, 'How have we come to this?', *Trouble & Strife*, 19 April 2016 http://www.troubleandstrife. org/2016/04/how-have-we-come-to-this/; Pragna Patel, 'The Sharia debate in the UK: who will listen to our voices?', openDemocracy, 14 December 2016, https://www. opendemocracy.net/5050/pragna-patel/sharia-debate- who-will-listen-to-us; and Ayelet Shachar, 'Entangled: family, religion and human rights', in Cindy Holder and David Reidy, eds, *Human Rights: The Hard Questions* (Cambridge University Press, 2013), pp. 115–35.

3. WORK

On the class, race and sexual politics of paid domestic labour, see Bridget Anderson, *Doing the Dirty Work* (Zed Books, 2000).

Amartya Sen's article 'More than 100 million women are missing' (*New York Review of Books*, 20 December 1990) is at http://www.nybooks.com/articles/1990/12/20/ more-than-100-million-women-are-missing/

Barbara Ehrenreich's *Nickel and Dimed* (Granta Books, 2002) investigates the reality of life for women working in low-paid, female-dominated occupations.

Katrine Marçal's *Who Cooked Adam Smith's Dinner?* (Portobello Books, 2015) is an accessible discussion of the male-centredness of economics. (The answer to the question posed in the title is: 'his mother' – and she did it for love, not money.)

4. FEMININITY

Two classic feminist treatments of femininity are Susan Brownmiller, *Femininity* (Simon & Schuster, 1984) and Naomi Wolf, *The Beauty Myth* (Chatto & Windus 1990). A more recent one is Emer O'Toole, *Girls Will Be Girls* (Orion, 2015).

Cordelia Fine's *Delusions of Gender* (Icon Books, 2010) and Angela Saini's *Inferior* (Fourth Estate, 2017) offer accessible feminist accounts of the science of sex and gender differences.

Bronwyn Davies's study of pre-school children acquiring gender is *Frogs and Snails and Feminist Tales* (Hampton Press, 2002). The gender diarists Ros Ball and James Millar have published a book about their experiences as parents, *The Gender Agenda* (Jessica Kingsley Publishers, 2017).

A lecture given in 2015 by Heather Widdows can be viewed online at http://www.birmingham.ac.uk/generic/beauty/news/2015/why-beauty-matters.aspx.

Julia Serano's analysis of femininity is laid out in *Whipping Girl* (Seal Press, 2007). For some reflections on the construction of masculinity, see Grayson Perry, *The Descent of Man* (Penguin, 2016).

5. SEX

The statement I quote on p. 86 from Carole Vance comes from the introduction to her edited volume *Pleasure and Danger* (Routledge, 1984). Lynne Segal writes about the feminist politics of pleasure in *Straight Sex* (Verso, 2015).

Anne Koedt's classic 1970 essay 'The myth of the vaginal orgasm' is available online at https://wgs10016.commons.gc.cuny.edu/the-myth-of-the-vaginal-orgasm-by-anne-koedt-1970/

Peggy Orenstein's *Girls and Sex* (HarperCollins, 2016) offers a snapshot of adolescent girls' sexual experiences in twenty-first-century America.

Porn culture is the subject of Ariel Levy, *Female Chauvinist Pigs* (Pocket Books, 2006). Kate Harding's *Asking For It* (Da Capo Press, 2015) deals with the phenomenon of rape culture.

A clear presentation of the feminist argument against prostitution can be found in Kat Banyard's *Pimp State* (Faber & Faber, 2016). For the opposing argument, see Laurie Penny's *Meat Market* (Zero Books, 2011).

Adrienne Rich's essay 'Compulsory heterosexuality and lesbian existence' is reprinted in the *Journal of Women's History* 15(3), Autumn 2003, pp. 11–48. On the experiences of lesbian women in Britain both before and during the feminist era, see Rebecca Jennings, *A Lesbian History of Britain* (Greenwood World Publishing, 2007).

Lisa Downing's thoughts on 'sex critical' feminism can be found on her blog, at http://sexcritical.co.uk/2012/07/27/what-is-sex-critical-and-why-should-we-care-about-it/

6. CULTURE

Originally published in 1929, Virginia Woolf's *A Room of One's Own* (Penguin Modern Classics, 2002) was based on lectures she had given in Cambridge the year before on the subject of 'women and fiction'. Alice Walker's 1974 essay 'In search of our mothers' gardens' can be read online at http://www.msmagazine.com/spring2002/walker.asp. The text of Susanna White's 2017 Fulbright lecture 'A screen of our own' is available at https://www.directors.uk.com/news/a-screen-of-one-s-own-a-fulbright-lecture-by-susanna-white.

Information on women composers is taken from Anna Beer, *Sounds and Sweet Airs: the Forgotten Women of Classical Music* (Oneworld Publications, 2016). Catherine Nichols's story, 'Homme de plume: what I learned sending my novel out under a male name', is at https://jezebel.com/homme-de-plume-what-i-learned-sending-my-novel-out-und-1720637627

The episode of *Ways of Seeing* that deals with the representation of women can be viewed on YouTube at https://www.youtube.com/watch?v=m1GI8mNU5Sg. The book version is John Berger, *Ways of Seeing* (Penguin Books, 1972). Laura Mulvey's essay on the male gaze appears in many anthologies, but the original version is Laura Mulvey, 'Visual pleasure and narrative cinema', *Screen* 16(3), Autumn 1975, pp. 6–18. On racism, the white gaze and the representation of Black women, see T. Denean Sharpley-Whiting, *Black Venus* (Duke University Press, 1999) and bell hooks, *Black Looks: Race and Representation* (Routledge, 2015).

An insightful discussion of the alt-right's tactic of waging culture war on feminism is Angela Nagle's book *Kill All Normies* (Zero Books, 2017).

7. FAULTLINES AND FUTURES

For a succinct discussion of the challenges facing feminists around the world (though it pre-dates the most recent developments), see Beatrix Campbell, *End of Equality*

(Seagull Books, 2014). Laurie Penny's 'How to be a genderqueer feminist' is available at https://www.buzzfeed.com/lauriepenny/how-to-be-a-genderqueer-feminist

Sylvia Walby's *The Future of Feminism* (Polity Press, 2011) is an academic assessment of the state of feminism in the second decade of the twenty-first century; Kira Cochrane's *All the Rebel Women* (Guardian Shorts, 2013) is a non-academic survey of the British 'fourth wave'.

The commodification of feminism is discussed in Andi Zeisler, *We Were Feminists Once* (PublicAffairs, 2016).

ACKNOWLEDGEMENTS

I am grateful to all the feminists whose collective wisdom I have learnt from over the years. Thanks to Marina Strinkovsky and Teresa Baron, and special thanks to my best critic, Meryl Altman.

INDEX

IDEAS IN PROFILE
SMALL INTRODUCTIONS TO BIG TOPICS

Ideas in Profile is a landmark series that offers concise and entertaining
introductions to topics that matter.

ALREADY PUBLISHED

The Ancient World Jerry Toner
Art in History Martin Kemp
Conservatism Roger Scruton
Criticism Catherine Belsey
Geography Carl Lee and Danny Dorling
Music Andrew Gant
Politics David Runciman
Shakespeare Paul Edmondson
Social Theory William Outhwaite
Theories of Everything Frank Close
Truth Simon Blackburn

FORTHCOMING

Language Alexandra Aikhenvald
Socialism Mark Stears